Dearest Carmelite Sisters

Miles Apart

With much love,
Agnes B Cagney

Miles Apart

As I Remember My Irish Childhood . . .
from There to Here—A Memoir

Agnes B. Cagney

VANTAGE PRESS
New York

FIRST EDITION

Copyright © 2006 by Agnes B. Cagney

Published by Vantage Press, Inc.
419 Park Ave. South, New York, NY 10016

Manufactured in the United States of America
ISBN: 0-533-15445-6

Library of Congress Catalog Card No.: 2006920347

0 9 8 7 6 5 4 3 2 1

With gratitude to my husband, Jack;
Daughters: Joan and Christine;
Grandchildren: Brian, Siobhan, Jackie,
Deirdre, Tyler, and Ethan;
Nieces: Angela and Grainne;
My dear friend, Frances,
whose love and encouragement have guided me.

Contents

Miles Apart

One

The Early Years

This Is My Letter

This is my letter to the world
That never wrote to me—
The simple news that Nature told
With tender majesty.
—Emily Dickinson

I was born toward the end of the 1930s and grew up on a farm in rural Ireland a few miles distant from the town of Mohill, County Leitrim, in northwest Ireland. Our house, which was situated atop a hillock up a short lane, over-looked green fields as far as the eye could see, rendered a feeling of openness and airiness. It consisted of the scullery or outside kitchen, the main kitchen, the parlor, and three bedrooms upstairs. The scullery was the work area where my mother prepared and cooked our food, plucked the freshly killed chickens for Sunday's dinner, and did the laundry. The main kitchen served as the living area where we gathered around the open fire for conversation, to pray the rosary, eat our meals, and do our homework. It was the central hub of activity in our home. The parlor, which was off limits to us children, was the formal room in our house. It was used on very special occasions like when we hosted the Station, that unique occasion when the priest came to our house to celebrate Mass; when we had visitors from America; and for serving meals during a wake.

In those days, country farmhouses did not have electricity, central heating, running water or indoor plumbing and indeed ours was no exception. It was a stately, two-storey structure built for my mother and father when they got married in the early 1930s. Today, this original house is unrecognizable to latecomers. While still a stately structure, with rows of daffodils on either side of the path leading to the front door, it has been extensively renovated and updated to include the amenities and comforts of most twenty-first-century residences.

Farmers did not measure their farms in terms of acreage, but referred to them as the number of cows' place in the holding, indicating the amount of land needed to comfortably feed and support a fixed number of livestock. In our case, our home farm, as we called it, contained about 40 acres and was contiguous to our house. There crops were sown and milking cows and young calves kept—all within my father's line of vision. In addition, my family owned another 30-plus acre farm a few miles away that was used for grazing and meadow land. It did not need much of my father's attention or intervention. The grass grew without help and the animals grazing there did so until sated. Both holdings had been in my grandmother's family for generations up until the time my father and mother married. At that point, my father's bachelor uncle (my grandmother's brother), the ancestral owner, signed the property over to my father. A new house was built for the newlyweds adjacent to the original dwelling. My granduncle and his sister, my father's mother, a widowed woman who lived a distance away, sold her farm when my father married. He was the only child who did not follow his three sisters to America. He and my grandmother were very close and depended on each other. He was the father figure in their home because his father died when he was twelve years old and his three sisters emigrated when they were teenagers. Following the sale of my grandmother's property and the signing over of the original home to my father, she and my granduncle, her brother, moved into the new house when my parents married. While not an idyllic situation for a young bride, my mother never complained about her circumstances. I would now say, based on my own life experiences, she probably felt more like another child in an adult setting with two mature in-laws looking over her shoulder. Fortunately, the new house was spacious enough so they had their own separate bedrooms.

World War II (1939–1945) was rapidly escalating on the European continent, which created severe economic problems in Ireland. In the words of Charles Dickens on another era, "'Twas the best of times, 'twas the worst of times." Even though I was very young, I clearly remember basic necessities being in short supply during and immediately following those lean wartime years. Meat, groceries, and everyday staples were scarce and tightly rationed. My family was more fortunate than many other families in our area. It included my parents, then in their mid-thirties; my grandmother, in her seventies; my bachelor granduncle, also in his seventies; and seven children, ranging in age from newborn to ten years. Four more children would arrive later.

Since we were a large, young family, we qualified for government subsidized ration coupons. These coupons served as income and my parents used them to help cover the cost of household necessities and incidentals we either did not need or use. My mother often traded those unused coupons with neighbors to help meet mutual needs, which varied from household to household.

Each member of our household, regardless of age, was entitled to ration coupons. When coupons valid for a specific period and product were exhausted, our requirements were not always covered. In such instances, my mother traded them with our neighbors to fulfill our needs. My parents quite often needed additional coupons for flour, sugar, and paraffin oil. Flour, the basic staple for bread, was a major necessity in our house and the coupon allotment did not meet our need. Without the availability of flour, many a child would go to bed hungry. Of course, a cup of tea and a bowl of oatmeal tasted better with a pinch sugar added. The hanging paraffin oil lamp, over the kitchen table, was our only source of light during the long winter nights. Electricity was not an option until roughly ten years later. Daily chores and odd jobs, like bringing in turf for the overnight fire, washing potatoes for dinner the following day, and feeding the chickens and turkeys, were completed during daylight hours. Knitting, darning socks, sewing on buttons and patching clothing, and cobbling boots and shoes were done after dark under the glow of the lamp's light.

Having neighbors whose needs were different from ours was a blessing in disguise for my parents. Oftentimes, when our neighbor's coupon supply was exhausted, they needed additional coupons for cigarettes or tobacco, and other items my family rarely used. Even though the ration coupons were somewhat of a lifesaver, there were occasions when we did without soap, detergent, and other inedible, store-bought goods. These items did not qualify for ration coupons subsidy. Soap and detergent were considered luxuries or non-essentials. Many families in those days of rationing restrictions and limited finances were not only scantily clad, they were also poorly nourished.

Fortunately, my family was blessed to have milk and butter supplied daily by the herd of dairy cattle that produced enough milk for drinking and churning to make butter. On several occasions, my mother gave a block of freshly churned butter to our elderly neighbor, a widower, who lived with his adult, bachelor son in a thatched house surrounded by gooseberry bushes, apple trees, ditches, and whitehorn hedges at the top of the hill a short distance further up the lane from our house. Before entering the thicket that surrounded his house, it was worthwhile stopping for a few moments to pause and enjoy the breathtaking view of the surrounding countryside with Corn Hill, County Longford, to the north, Slieve an Iarainn (mountain) on the Fermanagh border to the south, and the purple heather in the bog below. Beyond the bog, green hills spiraled upward and sloped down toward the lake to the west. Lush green fields speckled with wild flowers adorned the pasture east toward our school.

My parents were very friendly with our neighbor, an old man who lived in the house hidden from view a short distance up the lane from our house. Indeed, when we children contracted ringworm, he often made the cure for us. It was not unusual to be exposed to ringworm while growing up on a farm and in close contact with livestock infected with the fungus. This elderly gentleman suffered from a "bad stomach." When he walked past our house to fetch a bucket of water from our spring well, he often stopped at the scullery door to ask my mother for a teaspoonful of baking soda, diluted in a glass of water. When she gave him the mixture, he gulped it down quickly to help relieve the buildup of indigestion he felt in his stomach. As soon as we children saw him coming, we immediately took off because we could not stand the sound of his loud belching when the baking soda mixture reached his stomach and diffused the accumulation of gas. As the old man belched and slobbered, he thanked my mother for the relief he felt. The baking soda mixture was merely a temporary palliative for a very serious stomach ailment that would claim his life a short time later.

On Saturday morning my mother, with the help of my sisters, washed our clothes in an old-fashioned laundry tub set upon a stool in the scullery. The water was heated in a big, black cast iron pot that hung from a crook over the open turf fire in the hearth. The soiled clothes were soaked in washing soda and brown carbolic soap and then scrubbed clean on a washboard. For me, this was backbreaking work and a job I oftentimes ran off outdoors to avoid. If one did not have the knack of grasping the clothes firmly, the washboard scratched the skin off unwary knuckles. Not only was it a laborious job to scrub the men's heavy work clothes, but when they became stained from a bleeding knuckle, it was all the more difficult to get the blood stains out. My father, on his way outdoors to tend to farmyard responsibilities, often used one of his favorite expressions when the laundry was being done. With a slight smirk and a twinkle in his eye, he would say, "Oh, Saturday's wash for Sunday's dash, is it?"

As the years passed, my mother switched wash day from Saturday to Monday. By doing so, she left the washed clothes hanging out on the line overnight without any shred of guilt. She would not leave the wash out overnight on a Saturday night because Sunday was strictly a day of rest and no servile work was done on the Sabbath Day under the pain of sin. Even though doing the laundry was a necessity, she never violated the third commandment: "Remember to keep holy the Sabbath day." This was truly a day of rest and relaxation in our house, with the adults relaxing, reading the newspaper, and listening to football matches on the radio when the battery was charged and the reception clear and static free. Relatives and neighbors usually stopped by for a visit on Sunday afternoons. I enjoyed when they visited and occasionally rubbernecked to eavesdrop on their conversations when they related how their children, my cousins, were doing in school. If they were doing really well, I would presume their parents were bragging, which made me all the more determined not to be outdone.

When I was very young and as far back as I can remember, my mother, when putting us children to bed, would sing a good night lullaby called "The Babes in the Woods." I can still hear her voice as she trilled:

Oh, my dear, do you know
How a long time ago
Two poor little children
Whose names I don't know
Were stolen away
On a fine summer's day
And left in the woods
As I heard people say.
They sobbed and they sighed
And they bitterly cried
And the poor little things
They lay down and died
And when they were dead
The robin so red

Brought strawberry leaves
And over them spread
And all the day long
She sang them this song
Poor babes in the woods
Poor babes in the woods
And won't you remember
The babes in the woods?

Each night we pleaded with her to sing that song over and over. We looked forward to bedtime and to "The Dead Babies" song, as we called it. Immediately upon completing the song, she began saying our night prayers. When we were a little older, we were allowed to join the rest of the family in praying the rosary. Many of us were too young and too restless to kneel and pay attention to this long prayer. The trimmings that followed were usually much longer than the rosary itself. My mother could not devote too much time to our bedtime preparation. She needed to tend to my grandmother, granduncle, and younger siblings before her day's work was done. There was always a baby or a little one to be taken care of. We were born approximately 15 to 18 months apart. She made sure the henhouse door was shut so the elusive fox would not get in and snatch one of her best laying hens or one of her promising young chickens. When we went to bed, she baked bread for breakfast, washed dishes, and completed several additional, unfinished jobs she hadn't had time to complete during the day. She often remarked that there were not enough hours in her day and that "a mother's work is never done."

In mid-June 1943, my mother decided it was time for my older sister Kathleen to go to school. She was eighteen months older than I was. She cried at the thought of going to school and I cried at the thought of not being able to go along with her. We were very close and spent a lot of time together playing hide and seek, dressing up in old clothes, wearing Grandma's shoes and glasses, and engaging in make-believe games and conversations. By school attendance standards, I was too young to attend. Fortunately, I was tall for my age, so my mother decided she would send the two of us off together without discussing my age. Instead, she decided to wait and see if the issue arose or the teacher asked. As it happened, the topic never came up.

In our house, the usual school attendance preparations made for a busy and exciting time. My mother went to town to purchase new school supplies and enough calico material to make our new dresses for school. Calico came in a greater variety of colorful prints than cotton and she loved bright, flowered patterns for her girls. In addition, she believed calico material would hold up better than cotton for washing and ironing. My mother instilled in us the importance of wearing clean clothing. She feared we might have an accident or some emergency that would involve being taken to a doctor or hospital. In her opinion, wearing clean clothing was just as important as our injury. She made sure our hair was clean, face and neck washed, and nails neatly trimmed. Finally, she gave us instruction on how to use an outhouse, the makeshift outdoor toilet that stood at the end of the playground behind the school.

For lunch on my first day at school, my mother prepared a slice of currant bread, buttered, and a Milk of Magnesia bottle filled with fresh, whole milk. Occasionally, we had a slice of raisin or treacle bread—all homemade, of course, and a delightful treat. Upon entering the classroom, the children placed their bottles of milk in front of the open fire to keep them warm until lunchtime. It was not unusual to notice several blue Magnesia bottles lined up in front of the fire. Each child marked his bottle for identification so as not to confuse it with one that might contain goat's milk, which was not infrequent.

The school building had neither indoor plumbing nor central heating. Plumbing consisted of the outhouse and the heat emanated from a turf fire that burned in each classroom during the winter months. We were warned that when using the outhouse, we should be very careful not to slip through the big round hole in the seat into the bottomless pit below. The waste from the outhouse was emptied a couple times a year. When that day arrived, no one was heard to ask the teacher, *"Bhfuil cead agam dul amach?"* (May I have permission to go out?), because it was off-limits.

The job of emptying the outhouse was reserved for a tinker who happened to stop by our school whenever he needed a few shillings. The schoolmaster engaged him to do the job and dispose of the contents. Needless to say, this was very messy work. The tinker used a galvanized bucket, which he lowered with a rope, and then carried the buckets full of sewage off to a nearby drain where it was washed away by the rain. The grass around and on the bank of the drain was always a lush shade of green. It took us a while to figure out why this was so. We had often heard the song "Forty Shades of Green" used to describe Ireland. Now we knew how one shade came about. When the outhouse was out of service that meant the children either had to refrain from relieving themselves or, if they couldn't, they sought out a private place, usually behind a dense shrub, preferably a whin (called gorse in other parts of the country) or a whitethorn bush.

Since there was no central heating in the school, each family supplied turf for the fire, which they transported by either ass and cart or ass and creels. When the turf was delivered, it was a perfect occasion to escape the classroom to unload it. This was a great distraction, stretched out as long as possible, with children bringing in one sod of turf at a time when they could easily have managed two or three. The job was prolonged to take advantage of spending time outdoors and away from the discipline and restriction of the classroom.

Children going to school for the first time reported in early June. The academic year ended in mid-July when school closed until late August for summer holidays. Allowing children to attend school for a couple of weeks was a more gentle way of introducing them to a learning environment. By the end of August, when the new school year began, they knew what to expect and were ready for fulltime education. The school environment and experience had already been shared and they were somewhat familiar with the daily classroom routine.

On our way to school, we took advantage of a shortcut through the fields instead of walking an additional two miles, a challenging trip for a four-year-old, like me, when we took the road. We quickly learned how to avoid getting stuck in the slough, a wet stretch of marshland that ran through the fields we crossed. These walks, I believe, prepared us for the hardships life would surely deal us later on. We knew where the frog spawn and the newborn hedgehogs were incubating. Oftentimes we stopped by the edge of the river to look over the frog spawn nestled among the rushes and watched the little tadpoles swim to and fro. We were amazed at how fast they could move when all that we could see was a little eye and a short tail. They did not resemble frogs at all. As the tadpoles matured, the tail disappeared, their bodies grew wider, their heads took shape, and a second eye appeared, as well as gills, arms, and legs. In what seemed like no time at all, they were leaping from place to place and growing more rapidly each day. The mother hedgehog secured her babies under her quills so tightly that all we could see was her alone. Outdoor experiences, such as these, coupled with long walks through the countryside, were all part of our childhood and schooldays. These local schools are long since closed and replaced with regional schools. Students are transported by either school bus or automobile. No longer do children tarry by the riverbank to observe the frog spawn, tadpoles, and birds' nests. Today, it's unheard of for children to walk three or four miles each way to attend school. These events and memories remain with you through life. Nothing compares to seeing the wonder of nature unfold before your eyes.

My first exposure to infant class was learning the alphabet in both English and Irish. The teacher, a middle-aged lady, or so I thought (to a five-year-old, anyone over 20 looked old), started each day with the Sign of the Cross. Some children had difficulty getting the hang of making it and weren't sure whether the Holy Ghost was assigned to the right shoulder or the left. My sister had a particularly difficult time following the directions. She was left-handed and did not use her right hand to make the Sign of the Cross. The teacher would get very angry at her and insist that she learn to make it the correct way. After some time and practice she mastered doing it with her right hand. A greater problem arose when she was introduced to writing. She could not grip the pencil securely in her right hand. I remember the teacher whacking her across the knuckles with the side of the ruler for holding the pencil in her left hand. Every time she got hit, she would cry. I would cry, too, because I felt her pain. The teacher insisted she use her right hand just like everyone else in the room. After much practice and absolute fear, she mastered using her right hand while in school, but the moment she came home, she automatically used her left hand for everything else.

In class, I wrote on a slate with chalk to practice making letters and learning the alphabet. Each child had his own slate, which was roughly one square foot. When I mastered writing with chalk on the slate, I moved on to using a pencil. When I reached the higher classes, I used a pen with a nib dipped in the inkwell at the top of my desk. The mistress used a fountain pen to correct our school work. Owning a fountain pen was a rarity. Only the wealthier town folk like the doctor and vet could afford such a luxury. Ball point pens, felt tip pens, highlighters, and magic markers were not available until many years later.

In school we played with marla (also know as plasticine) and colored beads, made from painted spools, strung from side to side within a wooden frame and anchored securely at both ends. Plasticine was a pliable chunk or ball of rubber-like substance. When we rolled it between our hands it became soft and could be broken into small pieces to create figures and shapes of various sizes and styles. Many children were quite creative in making life-like reproductions and abstract sculptures. We used the colored spools for counting and simple addition and subtraction.

Our schoolhouse was a two-room stucco building with a black slate roof. The mistress taught infant, first, and second class. Since my sister was older than I was, she was moved to second class when school reopened in

August and I was moved to first class. In first class, we learned new prayers, Irish words, simple math problems, and reading, using the *Kincora Reader*. The mistress taught us words, phrases, and prayers including the Our Father, Hail Mary, and the Glory Be, in both English and Irish. We learned them through a combination of repetition, listening well, and a whole lot of fear. She conducted singing lessons and prepared the choir to sing hymns at Mass and on confirmation day. The schoolmaster was not a singer. It was said he couldn't carry a tune in a bucket. During singing practice, we listened to the sound of a tuning fork, which the mistress struck on the edge of a table, and then practiced singing the scale to the pitch of the tuning fork. That was a new experience as many of us did not know the difference between high notes and low notes. We learned many beautiful hymns and songs in both English and Irish. The better singers were usually placed front and center in the group with the lesser gifted mixed in to give the appearance of a large, talented group. The choir sang hymns at devotions, holy hours, benediction, and, confirmation.

The mistress taught us how to thread a needle and tie a knot as well as the basics of needlework and what she called the running stitch, that stitch commonly used when sewing straight seams and making hems. Later on, when we had mastered those basics, she taught us many different stitches including button hole, backstitching, the blanket stitch, and how to create a run-and-fell seam. In the higher classes, we secured samples of our work into a book that was examined by the sewing inspector who visited our school every couple of years. Having the inspector accept our work was the measure of the mistress's skill at teaching the class how to sew.

When we mastered sewing, the mistress taught us

how to knit using two knitting needles. The first assignment was learning to cast on stitches. As we progressed, she taught us the plain garter stitch, the purl stitch, and so on until we mastered following a pattern, which we eventually did when we were more skilled in reading and following written directions. The true test of our ability to follow a pattern was measured by our ability to knit using four needles to create a pair of socks and excel at the process of turning the heel. When we accomplished those tasks, we made mittens, gloves, and sweaters.

About halfway through my first class year, a new student, an eight-year-old boy, joined our class. He was the son of a very poor, local farmer who had not started school at the usual age of six because he did not have suitable school clothing. At home, he wore his father's old shirts and trousers with the sleeves and legs cut off to render a reasonable fit. He probably would not have started at eight if the local police had not come to his house to advise his parents they were in violation of the law and warning them their son would be a candidate for the Industrial School if they did not immediately enroll him in school. This dreaded, prison-like facility, the Industrial School, was where contemptuous students were sent to be rehabilitated when they violated laws or engaged in unacceptable behavior like juvenile delinquency.

Our mistress was a talented knitter and upon hearing about his situation, she knitted him a lovely green long-sleeved gansey (pullover) so he could start school. In class one day, she noticed that its cuffs were black and crusty because he used them to wipe his runny nose. Every day, he wore his green pullover, until it was worn beyond repair. Since he lived in a one-room, mud floor house, he wasn't exposed to life beyond its walls except on those occasions when he played and ran through the fields with his shaggy dog. Before starting school, personal appearance was not important to either him or his parents.

It distressed our mistress to see this boy regularly use the cuffs of the sweater as a handkerchief. To solve the problem and extend the life of the sweater's cuffs, she gave him a handkerchief to use when he felt the need to blow his nose. Since he had never used a handkerchief before, or had never seen one used, he had no idea how it worked. Our mistress directed him to use it each time he needed to blow his nose. When an occasion arose, he unfolded the handkerchief and spread it out over the palm of his open, left hand. Then, taking his right hand, he reached for his snotty nose, pinched both nostrils tightly and gave a great blow onto the open handkerchief spread out on the palm of his left hand. When that was done he did not know what to do with the used handkerchief. The mistress demonstrated for him how he should properly use a handkerchief and when used told him to return it to his pocket. Nowadays, we tend to forget the handkerchief replaced the cuff, the disposable tissue replaced the handkerchief, and, if a tissue wasn't available, a wad of toilet paper was substituted to perform the task. When the boy returned to school the day following the handkerchief lesson, he had a question for both the teacher and the entire class. It was a message from his father, who had asked his son to ask everyone: "What is it that a poor man throws away and a rich man puts in his pocket?" We were all stumped searching for an answer, as was the mistress. When no one knew the answer, the boy took delight in telling us it was a snot.

After completing first class, I was promoted to second class, which was a much more challenging year. In our area, school levels were measured by the class a student was in. Other areas called them grades. As a second class student that meant I was now either seven years old or soon to be, which indicated I had reached the age of reason. At that age, I was expected to have attained the level of maturity to distinguish between right and wrong. I was taught how to prepare for First Confession and First Holy Communion. Once a week, the local parish priest came to our school and asked questions about sin, if I disobeyed our parents, used bad language, told lies, stole anything, missed Mass on Sundays or holy days of obligation, or ate meat on Fridays, which was a sin breaching one of the commandments of the Church. That practice of abstaining from meat on Friday was abandoned as a result of the Second Vatican, in the early 1960s. He instructed us in the preliminaries of how to properly prepare for confession and the importance of being in the state of grace to receive our First Holy Communion. He would talk very seriously about the consequences of breaking any of the Ten Commandments, sins—both venial and mortal—the eternal happiness of heaven, temporary stays in Purgatory, Limbo (that unknown place of punishment for stillborn babies and un-baptized children), and the everlasting damnation of Hell, out of which there was no redemption. In our area children were baptized a day or two after they were born. Teaching children about Limbo was also discontinued following the Second Vatican Council. Not a mention of it since then. No discussion, but many questions asked about whatever happened to those who either went to Limbo or ate meat on Fridays prior to the Second Vatican Council.

Words like mortal and venial were new to my limited vocabulary. I was often terrified trying to differentiate between them. Religion was serious business indeed, especially when it came from the mouth of the priest.

17

Upon hearing the priest's interpretation and definition of sin, I soon recognized many of the expressions and slang words I grew up with and often used qualified as sins. My great challenge was to distinguish whether they were mortal or venial. Naturally, I hoped they were venial sins, which meant I did not have to confess them. Mortal sins, on the other hand, were much more serious and warranted confessing. For a sin to be mortal, it must have grave matter, full knowledge, and full consent. Furthermore, all three must be present at the same time. Thus, these components indeed provoked a lot of thought raising the question if all three were present at once. What if only two were? In my confusion, I honestly didn't believe seven-year-olds were capable of committing mortal sins, so my next challenge was to classify the sins in the hope that the list would be neither too long nor too short. It was not uncommon to make up a few sins to be sure the number seemed reasonable and acceptable to the priest. That decision presented the problem of maybe having to fudge the numbers in such a way not to lie in confession and commit the even graver sin of sacrilege.

Before I made my First Confession and First Holy Communion, I was required to know the meaning of mortal and venial sins as defined in the *Short Catechism*, a booklet of questions and answers. These definitions, and only these—no interpretations or substitutions—were drilled into our heads until we could repeat them without a moment's hesitation. "Mortal sin is a grievous offense or transgression against the law of God. Venial sin is a less grievous offense or transgression against the law of God." As a seven-year-old, these definitions were difficult to comprehend and put into everyday practice. I had no idea what transgressions or grievous offenses were, but I knew they meant some serious stuff. My limited vocabulary and comprehension as well as my childhood innocence were not sophisticated enough to grasp their full impact and meaning.

The superstitions I grew up hearing and indeed sometimes practiced because that was the custom, seemed to fall under the category of sin. According to our local priest, I learned for the first time that superstition was a plea to the devil and should always be avoided. When I was fully prepared and knowledgeable in the required study of the *Short Catechism*, I was allowed to make my First Confession and receive First Holy Communion. Of course, the mistress warned me to appear at the church clean and tidy and wearing my very best clothes. This was exciting for me because I was the one with the new clothes to pass on to younger siblings rather than being the one to receive the hand-me-downs.

My First Confession was scheduled for eleven o'clock on the second Saturday in May at our local church. Our class met at school that morning. Together, we walked through the dew-covered fields up the byroad to the parish church for our First Confession. Since the church was about four miles from the school, I was tired when I got there. Once inside, I knelt down before the altar and said my preparatory prayers asking God for the grace to make a good confession. When that was done, the moment of reckoning was at hand, we each took our turn going into the confessional to make our First Confession. Once I got past the usual "Bless Me Father . . . " panic and fear took over as it was now time to confess my sins. Not knowing how the priest would react to what I was confessing, I was trembling with the fear of being recognized, or even worse, of having offended God and being condemned for my sins. Would the priest raise his voice for everyone in the church to hear and loudly chastise me for being such a sinner? I did not know what to expect. Only God could predict what our teacher would say and do if the priest raised his voice to one of her pupils. That being the case, I decided it was a good idea not to shock the priest and keep the sins to as few in number as possible, always emphasizing the venial ones and muttering the serious sins in muted tones slightly above a whisper.

Immediately following my confession and saying my penance, it was time for the long walk back home. About a mile from the church, we all sat down on a grassy knoll along the roadside and together we went over the sins we had just told to the priest. Some of us shared how we sometimes told lies, disobeyed our parents a few times, and so on. One of the boys related how he told the priest he had lied about a thousand times, had disobeyed his parents several hundred times, and had said curse words hundreds of times. In reenacting his confession, he used the actual curse words to describe what he told the priest.

By the time I got home from the church, it was time to start getting ready for the next day and my First Holy Communion. For me, my First Holy Communion was a bittersweet occasion. It was a rainy, windy day. Due to the severe weather, I could not join my classmates to receive First Holy Communion as a group in our home parish. You see, our house was situated in the outer limits of our home parish. We lived much closer to the next parish and that was where my family attended Mass, went to confession, devotions, holy hours, benediction, missions, novenas, and other church-related services and activities. It was in this parish that I received my First Holy Communion.

While disappointed that I could not receive it in my home parish, I nevertheless had an exciting day. I arose early that Sunday morning, got washed, dressed, and ready for the long walk to church for seven-thirty morning Mass while fasting from the night before, which was the rule at that time. As I walked along, I remember repeating to myself over and over again, "Don't destroy it in your mouth." The mistress had warned me and all the First Communicants on several occasions that we should swallow the Sacred Host as soon as the priest placed it on our tongue. She cautioned us every day with the same "Don't destroy it in your mouth" message. She repeatedly said that the priest's consecrated hands and our sin-free tongues were the only objects that could touch Holy Communion. I can still visualize her standing up in front of our class and repeating over and over again, "Don't destroy it in your mouth." If the Sacred Host got stuck to the roof of your mouth, which it usually did, you were supposed to somehow wiggle your tongue around and around to release it and then swallow it as quickly as possible.

I did not have the pleasure of wearing a white communion dress and I think that was the main reason why my mother did not want me to make my First Holy Communion in our home parish even though it was not appropriate weather for a white dress. Nevertheless, I recall thinking how everybody in the church would know I was wearing new clothes, brand new white socks, and white canvas shoes. The smell of the camphor from the new coat my father bought in town was still strong. Dad shopped for us on either a market or fair day when he had money from the sale of either pigs, calves, or other livestock. He did most of our clothes shopping including our winter coats. My mother bought our undergarments and material for our dresses, which she made by hand. In those lean years following World War II, my practical and conscientious parents did their best with what they could afford and we were always dressed neatly and sensibly.

When First Holy Communion was over, the remainder of the second grade was a time to receive the sacraments regularly, learn more prayers, and go to monthly confession. In addition, the teacher taught me how to prepare for and celebrate major holydays. I learned how to make a St. Brigid's cross for February 1st, her feast day. St. Brigid was the first Irish female saint. The cross was made from rushes, interwoven into the shape of a cross. For St. Patrick's Day, I gathered shamrock, which I wore to Mass securely pinned on my lapel. Also, as a ritual every year immediately before St. Patrick's Day, I collected fresh shamrock, which my parents mailed to family members abroad replete with *Beannachtaí Na Féile Pádraig* (Blessings of St. Patrick) greetings. St. Patrick's Day and Christmas were the two special occasions when greetings were sent to friends and relatives at home and abroad. On May 1st, I gathered primroses and cowslips, the most abundant and readily available wild spring flowers, and respectfully placed them in front of statues of Mary to honor her during the month May, her month, and at the entrance to the houses I encountered on my way to school.

When it was time to buy us children new shoes, my father drew an outline of our feet on a piece of strong, brown paper and carefully cut around it resulting in a facsimile of an insole. If we did not have brown paper in the house, he used a piece of twine to measure the length of our feet from toe to heel. He took both the foot outline and the piece of twine to the shoe store, where he checked for shoe sizes until he found a solid, sensible shoe that would freely accommodate the homemade insole. Coupled with the twine measurement, this was a more convenient way of buying shoes that fit than transporting us to the shoe store, a distance of over four miles away. He usually added a tad extra to the measurement to allow room for growing feet. My mother, being a gentle, mild-mannered woman, left the shopping up to my father, a very astute shopper who did not fail to make a bargain and strike a deal. My mother would have been embarrassed to negotiate prices. She was always happy when she talked my father into the job of shopping for the more expensive items like shoes and heavy coats.

Another government benefit for large families was subsidy coupons that could be applied toward the purchase of boots, shoes, and knee-high waterproof boots called wellingtons. As children, we were delighted because that meant we got new footwear every year. When the soles of our shoes wore out before the year was up, my father, being a worthwhile cobbler, purchased squares of leather and replaced the soles and heels which made the shoes as good as new and extended their wear. On other occasions, he removed the uppers from worn out soles and replaced the sole with wooden clog soles. These clogs were difficult to get used to because the rigid, wooden soles did not bend while walking. Many years later, clogs were the fashion craze among teenagers. Little did we know at the time our talented and visionary father was years ahead of his time in the world of style. My father bought our heavy coats in larger sizes to render a couple extra years' wear before they were passed down to the next child. Many times I felt cheated being the third girl in the family because by the time I got the hand-me-downs, they were usually well worn.

Another financial benefit to my family was the children's allowance. This rather modest government program subsidized the income of families with children.

The two oldest did not receive an allowance, but subsequent children did. That was an enormous assistance to large families because the more children they had the more financial subsidy they received. Even though it was not an overly generous financial allocation, it was helpful to my parents, who used it cautiously to cover the cost of groceries for our household and clothing for us children.

When I was eight years old, my mother brought me along with her to a neighbor's wake, a 95-year-old woman who was reposing in her home, as was the custom. I had never been to a wake before and had no idea what awaited me or what I should expect. Customarily, when women entered the house of a deceased person, they went directly to the room where the deceased was reposing. My mother ushered me along by her side and we, too, went to the room where the wake was taking place. There we came face to face with death. This was a first experience for me. The old lady was laid out in the upper room of their small, thatched house. I don't know why it was called the upper room as there were only three rooms in the entire house. Another was the parlor and the third was the kitchen *cum* sitting room, which was large enough to serve as both an eating area and place to relax on the sofa and armchairs neatly arranged around the open turf fire. When we entered the upper room, we knelt down at the foot of the bed and said a prayer for the repose of the old lady's soul. We then walked alongside the bed and shook the hand of the deceased. I did not want to touch the deceased, but custom had it that if you did not touch the flesh of a deceased person, you would be haunted by that person for the rest of your life. I surely did not want any of that, so with the security of my mother holding my free hand I bravely and barely touched the deceased in one quick motion. It was also said that if you touched a dead person, you would be granted an indulgence and the dead person would not come to you in your dreams. The departed soul would surely rest in peace.

For me, this was a ghostly sensation filled with a strange, unusual fear. I remember feeling scared the very moment I saw the little old lady laid out in her brown shroud with its hood strings tied snugly under her chin. Her hands were clasped as if in prayer and rosary beads were entwined through her gnarled, arthritic fingers. There she lay with her eyes closed as if she were sleeping. Her face was pale and ashen. When we said our good-bye, we took our seats along the bedroom wall. It was the custom in our area to never leave the corpse alone. Someone was expected to remain in the room until another mourner arrived. I was hoping and praying that some other people would soon come along so I could get out of there as quickly as possible.

During the waiting period, a member of the family passed snuff around. Not knowing what it was, I took a big snort and sneezed for about 15 minutes until finally my mother took me outside in the fresh air. Being only about eight years of age, I had never sampled snuff before and, since this was my first wake, I did not realize what a sniff of snuff could do. When I recovered and came back inside, my mother and I were invited to the parlor for a modest meal, followed by a glass of sherry and biscuits for the women and dessert for everyone. This was a pleasant treat, as I desperately needed a change of scenery as well as something to get rid of the effects of the snuff. The meal consisted of ham, lettuce, tomatoes, Chef's sauce, loaf bread, butter, and jam. When I finished eating, I was delighted to see the lady of the house break out the dessert, which was a lovely serving of red Bird's Jelly Deluxe. My mouth was watering as I watched her serve it. It seemed as if it would not come my way soon enough. When I was finally served, I could not believe that this lovely red slippery stuff did not need any chewing. You see, it was the first time I ever had jelly. We occasionally had custard, corn flour, oatmeal, or rice pudding—never jelly. When I finished eating this treat, I picked up my bowl and licked it clean. I recall my mother telling me it was bad manners to lick a plate. On our way home from the wake, she stressed the importance of good manners, especially in company. I just could not bear the thought of wasting even the tiniest morsel. Good manners aside, Bird's Jelly was the most delightful thing I had ever tasted and it helped get rid of the effects of the snuff.

The old lady's funeral was held the day following the removal. Early that morning, the local farmers dug the grave. A grave was not dug the day before because legend had it that it should not remain open overnight for fear the fairies would haunt it. Relatives, near and distant, neighbors, and those who wanted to see and be seen attended the funeral. The popularity of the deceased was measured in proportion to the size of his or her funeral so it was very important to have a good showing present for the final farewell.

As soon as the funeral service was over—in some cases a Mass, in others the Office of the Dead or a final blessing—neighborhood men acted as pallbearers and carried the coffin on their shoulders from the church to the graveyard. The chief mourners, usually the immediate family and close relatives, took their place behind the coffin. The remaining folks walked in procession behind them. When the funeral procession entered the graveyard, everyone proceeded very cautiously to the newly dug grave site making sure no one tripped or fell along the way. In our part of the country, legend had it that if you fell in a graveyard, you were destined to be the next one buried there. Needless to say, the people attending the funeral carefully picked and chose where they placed their feet for fear they would trip and, God forbid, fall down. Later on in life, I came to realize that this was nothing more than a threat used to prevent children from playing games or showing disrespect within and around a graveyard. It worked very well indeed.

Following a burial, it was customary to go to a pub for some refreshment. Funerals were community events. Relatives and neighbors exchanged messages of sympathy to the survivors with a handshake, followed by the usual "Sorry for your trouble." Following these courtesies, the men partook in a pint or two of Guinness at the bar nearby while the women repaired to the back room for biscuits, soft drinks, and occasionally a glass of sherry. Conversation always evolved around the life of the deceased, and even if he or she had lived to reach a hundred years, you would hear comments about the deceased dying at a young age and how great the loss.

My mother often told us that it was not good to bemoan or carry on after the death of a loved one, saying, "God had called that person home and if you don't freely let him or her go to God, their soul would not rest in peace." There was a very thin line between grieving and crying openly following the death of a loved one. Sadness and grief were common mourning emotions that demonstrated a deep personal loss. If a person did not show any feelings of loss or emotion, he was considered hardhearted, which implied he or she was relieved that the person had passed on. Even when the death was a profound tragedy, such as that of a young child or the parent of a young family, it was much more important that their soul should rest in peace and not suffer any torture because those left behind did not willingly accept God's command when He called them home to eternal life with Himself. People rarely wept openly or publicly and never questioned God's plan, as they feared by doing so they would torture the departed soul and it might not rest in peace. Instead, they went about their daily business with heavy hearts mourning in silence.

> Oh, breathe not his name, let it sleep in the shade
> Where cold and unhonor'd his relics are laid,
> Sad, silent, and dark be the tears that we shed,
> As the night-dew that falls on the grass o'er his head!
> But the night-dew that falls, though in silence it weeps,
> Shall brighten with verdure the grave where he sleeps,
> And the tear that we shed, though in secret it rolls,
> Shall long keep his memory green in our souls.
> —Moore's Irish Melodies

Weeping and lamenting usually took place privately and behind closed doors or in the confines of one's own home. It was customary for members of the immediate family to arrange and attend a Month's Mind Mass for the deceased. As a sign of mourning, women wore a black arm band and men a black diamond-shaped patch on their sleeve. These outward symbols were worn for a year following the death of a loved one. Mourners did not attend parties, dances, or other social events during the year following the burial of relatives. This tradition has long since passed and is no longer observed. Nowadays, the life and good deeds of the deceased are what we remember and rejoice in.

Two

Schoolmaster Days

There Is No Frigate Like a Book

There is no frigate like a book
To take us lands away,
Nor any coursers like a page
Of prancing poetry.
—Emily Dickinson

Following the completion of second grade, I was promoted to third and introduced to the schoolmaster who taught third through eighth grades. He was a tall, bald-headed man who possessed a great love of poetry, the Irish language, and history. It was a major change for me from a frizzy-haired mistress to look at an ashen faced, bald-headed man as he steadily stared out over the classroom or unexpectedly asked a student a question. This was his way of making sure everyone was alert and not day-dreaming. He would be our teacher for the next six years in our two-room schoolhouse. Low infants, high infants, and first and second grades were taught by the mistress and housed in the adjoining classroom.

Our school had a combined enrollment of roughly 40 students. The majority were supplied by three large families in the area who had several school-age children. On many occasions, children from one of these families were in successive classes. Having an older sibling in a higher class was both an advantage and a disadvantage. An advantage was when the older sibling was promoted to the next highest class; the books he or she used were passed on, saving parents the cost of books and other incidental necessities. Also, since the books were already in the household, it was a great opportunity for the upcoming sibling to become familiar with the material ahead of time and have an advantage over those who were not as fortunate to have had a preview of the upcoming school work. One major disadvantage was the fear of being compared to the sibling who already had completed the class and may have been smarter than the one that followed.

The remainder of the student body was composed of children from families within the district who either had one, two, or three children. Each grade was composed of five or six children all working on their assignments and lessons simultaneously. No two grades worked on the same assignment or subject at the same time. When one grade was practicing penmanship or doing math problems, another stood around one of the large wall maps studying either history or geography. A third group stood in a straight line at the rear of the classroom practicing recitation or reading from their textbooks.

Our schoolmaster had the ability to teach and instruct six or seven classes simultaneously and with ease. The daily schedule was arranged so that none of the classes ever conflicted or overlapped. As students, we often whispered to one another that he must have eyes in the back of his head because he never missed a beat—neither studies nor capers. The only time during the school day the entire student body engaged in common activity was at twelve noon, before lunch, when he led us in saying the Angelus, which he rendered in Irish. We looked forward to the Angelus because there were no clocks in the classroom and we knew once it was over, lunch and a half-hour's playtime followed. Punctually at one o'clock he tapped on the windowpane with his key, giving us the signal it was time to come back inside and continue our school work until dismissal at three o'clock. Afternoon lessons included the dreaded sums (math), followed by Irish, history, geography, and English. Sums were the biggest problem since there was no such thing as a calculator available in those days. In a moment of desperation, a peek at the answers in the *Answer Book* on the schoolmaster's large table in front of the fire didn't do any harm.

The challenge was selecting the appropriate time to sneak a peek and avoid getting caught by the schoolmaster. When time was running out and no appropriate opportunity was presenting itself, invariably one of the students would raise his hand telling him "I think I hear the sound of a car coming" or "Was that a knock at the door I just heard?" Just as soon as the master went outside to check, someone would make a mad dash to check the answers in the *Answer Book* and then discreetly pass them around to the other struggling students. Our schoolmaster was more interested in a student getting the correct answer rather than the method used to arrive at it. What a time-saver it was to get an occasional answer here and there without having to labor through all the time-consuming steps to arrive at it.

Our schoolmaster was born and educated in the west of Ireland and was fluent in the Irish language. He grew up in the *Gaeltacht*, that part of the west of Ireland where Irish (Gaelic) was his first language. Oftentimes, he reminded us that we did not share the Irish culture he knew and, that in fact, we did not have any culture at all.

Since we lived much further inland, we did not have the same exposure to the Irish language he was fortunate enough to grow up using. In addition, our parents did not speak or know any Irish because it was not a mandatory requirement in their schooldays just prior to the establishment of the Irish Free State when Ireland was under the rule of England. As we became proficient in Irish, it was fun to speak it among ourselves at home. My mother, not understanding what we were saying, would surmise we were up to some kind of devilment and innocently say, "Don't think you're fooling me, I know what you're up to," and, as all mothers in their wisdom know their children's antics all too well, invariably she was right.

Each morning the schoolmaster called the attendance roll. When a student's name was called out, he or she answered *an seo* (here). If there was no response, another student would respond *amach* (absent). In third grade, the schoolmaster taught math (sums), catechism, Irish grammar, Irish history and geography, poetry, readings in prose and fiction, as well as penmanship. In our math class he invariably used the example of a traveling salesman selling A number of B products at C pounds, shillings, and pence. This became even more complicated if ha'pennies, farthings, and multiples thereof were included. To complicate matters even more, he often used the example of paying for the products purchased with the money obtained from the sale of X dozen of eggs at Y shillings a dozen. We dreaded the problem solving period and decided it was the most despised period in the school day and often giggled among ourselves at the stupidity of those shoppers who tried to make something simple so complex. Why couldn't they just sell their eggs and pay for their stuff with the egg money instead of going around and around?

The schoolmaster sat facing the students at a long wooden table in front of the turf fire. The building had neither central heat nor running water. The only light available came through the long narrow windows on those intermittent occasions when the sun shone, which was indeed a rare occurrence in Ireland where the weather is both cloudy and wet. In the cold winter months, we often mumbled under our breath, complaining how he blocked the heat from reaching us chilled-to-the-bone children seated much further back in the classroom and distantly removed from the heat of the blazing fire that burned behind him. When a student had a cough or wet feet, he was invited to take a seat at the end of the schoolmaster's worktable adjacent to the open fire. Children oftentimes muffled their cough so as not to be invited to sit next to him. They rarely complained about being wet or having a cold because they did not want him to scrutinize their every move and hear their sighs.

The schoolmaster's limited wardrobe consisted of one or two tweed jackets, a maroon pullover, gray slacks, and brown slacks. His favorite jacket was brown tweed with leather patches on the elbows. He wore his Sunday best, a light gray suit, on the day the inspector came to question the children to establish if they qualified for promotion to the next higher grade. When he visited our school, we were on our best behavior and woe betide us afterward if we didn't render the correct answer when called upon.

On regular school days, the schoolmaster wore his tweed jacket with the leather patches on the elbows and brown slacks that were worn to a shine in various places. He gave the appearance of a gentleman and an authority figure, always wearing a white shirt and a red and black striped tie—trappings not usually worn by the local farmers, except on Sundays, or to attend a funeral or wedding.

Our nickname for the schoolmaster was "Yellow Bones" because his fingers were indelibly stained with nicotine from the Gold Flake cigarettes he smoked. That particular brand of cigarettes was packaged in a flat, yellow box, which was a perfect match for his yellow-tinted fingers and the class decided the nickname "Yellow Bones" seemed appropriate. That was the name by which he was sometimes affectionately, sometimes objectionably, but always secretly known.

Occasionally, when he either forgot his cigarette lighter or ran out of matches, he used a circular, convex piece of glass to capture the rays of the sun peering through the window. He held his cigarette close to the glass where the concentrated heat was powerful enough to light it. We marveled at his ingenuity and watched the process closely as he patiently waited for the swirl of smoke to drift upward from the lighted cigarette. With that accomplished, he walked back to his seat, puffed on the cigarette, and tipped the ashes into the fireplace behind him.

Each day he wrote a proverb on the blackboard, which we copied several times into our copybooks. This process served at least two purposes. The first to practice good penmanship; the second to grasp, and put into everyday practice the message and meaning of the proverb itself. Proverbs served as reminders into motives and conduct as well as a deeper understanding of some of the varied interests that stir the human heart. They form a kind of synthesis of national character and moral tendencies of a race; in our case, the Irish. One of his favorite proverbs was "Associate with the nobles, but be not cold to the poor or the lowly." Another day he wrote the proverb "Closing the door when the horse is gone." He then carefully selected one of the boys to explain its meaning, knowing this particular boy's father owned horses and was the most likely candidate to interpret the meaning. The boy was very confused and hesitantly answered, "I don't know why anyone would bother to close the door when there is no horse to keep safely inside." He said, "My father usually closed the door when the horse was in his stall, otherwise he left it wide open for ventilation." In sheer frustration, the schoolmaster would walk over to the statue of St. Patrick and say, "You can't make a silk purse out of a sow's ear." Then he would turn to the class and pronounce, "Reputation is more enduring than life." He loved rattling off some of his favorite proverbs like "No pain like that of refusal"; "The empty barrel makes the most noise"; "No heat like that of shame," and on and on, sputtering out a whole litany of adages, usually closing with "Character is better than wealth," or "A foot at rest meets nothing."

Proverbs ranked highly among his favorite topics and indeed he had a long list of them on the tip of his tongue ready to blurt out regardless of what subject he was teaching. He enjoyed discussing their meaning and sharing their interpretation with the class. I'm not sure what influence these old, trite, simple adages, had on my classmates, but for me they opened a door—a door I may never have gone through had it not been for him, a dedicated teacher who created an extraordinary setting where learning, for me, would be a fascinating experience. The truisms he frequently cited became a springboard to a discussion on life and he kept them coming at length. He had the ability to take an ordinary, everyday situation and turn it into an extraordinary, lifelong lesson.

As we moved along through the fourth and fifth grades, learning and instruction became more comprehensive and accelerated. We were exposed to and covered a wider range of subjects and topics. Homework assignments were more frequent and voluminous. By now, we were just about fluent in speaking and reading works in Irish. That made him quite happy. He was pleased to see how we were growing in the understanding and usage of the Irish language, our native tongue and his love.

A major addition to our usual lessons in fourth grade, was introducing us to Latin. Our first lesson was learning the responses given at Mass. (Prior to Vatican II, Mass was celebrated in Latin.) Learning the Latin responses, including the Confiteor, the Gloria, Creed, and the Our Father took several months to master. When we reached fifth grade, the boys who knew the responses without a moment's hesitation would serve as altar boys. Some students occasionally got a little confused between Irish and Latin because they had already learned the responses in Irish and were more fluent and familiar with that language. All the boys and girls were taught the Latin responses used at Mass even though, in those days, girls were not allowed to act as altar servers. The schoolmaster played the role of the priest and he randomly called on either a boy or a girl to render the appropriate response. He told us the reason he included girls was that in the event an occasion arose when no altar boy was available to give the Latin responses, a girl could do so from outside the altar rails. At that time, females were not allowed to enter the sanctuary, the area inside the altar rails.

In addition to the everyday classroom instruction and homework assignments, fifth grade included preparation for confirmation. This was a major responsibility; indeed a time when the effectiveness of the schoolmaster's teaching and students' learning of Christian doctrine would be put to the test. We studied hard, learning and reviewing both *Short and Long Catechisms* and Bible history, including both the Old and New Testaments. We memorized what was commanded and forbidden by the Ten Commandments of God and the six Commandments of the Church. These would form and serve as the foundation upon which we would build our code for life.

On Confirmation Day, our school was represented by one boy and one girl to stand attentively before the bishop for questioning on a broad range of Christian doctrine topics indicating the classes' preparedness for reception of the sacrament. These two children were the first to be confirmed. As it happened, I represented the girls and I recall being nervous, not knowing if the bishop would give me such a severe slap on my cheek that I might cry or lose my balance. The bishop gave a slap on the cheek because as the Catechism says, "To put you in mind that by Confirmation you are strengthened to suffer and if necessary even to die for Christ."

Some boys had scared us telling stories about how the bishop, who was usually a rotund man, could send you reeling across the aisle with such a severe blow on the cheek that you would go flying out the side door of the church and land alongside the tall, stone headstones that were erected over the graves of deceased former parish priests. Of course that never happened. The day of confirmation was a solemn and sacred occasion for the parish, the school, and indeed the entire community. The emphasis was on the bishop coming to the parish and administering the sacrament. The schoolmaster was the sponsor for the boys and the mistress for the girls. In many of the larger cities and towns, those being confirmed could choose their own sponsor. We were not granted that privilege. Fanfare was kept to the barest minimum. Any questions or decisions concerning or about confirmation were handled and made by the school teachers; parents and godparents did not matter.

Following the reception of the sacrament, our big treat of the day was a trip to the village to have our picture taken in our confirmation regalia. This was followed by a stop at the confectionery shop where we enjoyed the extravagant luxury of ice cream sundaes at a dainty, but quaint ice cream parlor at the edge of town.

As I progressed and was promoted from one grade to another until I had completed National School, I never ceased to be amazed at the amount of knowledge our schoolmaster carried in his rather small, bald head. He was one of the few men in our area who was bald. My father often chuckled when we described baldness. He fortunately was endowed with a thick head of hair and would tell us since the schoolmaster came from the rugged west of Ireland where stone walls were used for fences because bushes didn't grow there, he wasn't surprised that hair didn't grow there either.

Our remaining years in the more advanced, upper-level grades were spent learning algebra, geometry, European history, world geography, reading some of Shakespeare's plays, poetry and recitation, as well as building fluency in languages. To complete the school day, the schoolmaster used any remaining time touching upon myths and legends with particular emphasis on ancient Irish folklore and tales. He introduced us to French and considered it a major handicap if people could not understand or converse in more than one language. To him, it really did not matter very much if he was teaching a lesson in either English, Irish, mathematics, or history, invariably he threw in some French or Latin words and phrases to either clarify or make a point and, at the same time, to call attention to and understand the interchange of languages as well as to help the students build fluency. Nowadays, with Ireland a part of the European Union, it is necessary to have a command of, or at least, an understanding of French, Spanish, and German when communicating with those European countries on issues of trade and commerce.

Now that we had been introduced to Latin and had made sufficient progress in conversational French, he invariably returned to his deep love of poetry and recitation. One of his favorite poems was "The Deserted Village" by Oliver Goldsmith. He favored many others including "An Old Woman of the Roads" by Padraic Colum, "Dark Rosaleen" by James Clarence Mangan, "Elegy Written in a Country Church Yard" by Thomas Gray, "Trees" by Joyce Kilmer, and works by Jonathan Swift, W. B. Yeats, Thomas Moore and others. Invariably, he favored the works of Irish poets. "The Deserted Village" stands tallest in my memory. He often cited lines from it and likened it to a reasonable facsimile of himself—particularly the section where Goldsmith rendered:

There, in his noisy mansion, skill'd to rule,
The village master taught his little school;
A man severe he was, and stem to view;
I knew him well, and every truant knew;
Well had the boding tremblers learn'd to trace
The day's disasters in his morning face;
Full well they laugh'd with counterfeited glee,
At all his jokes, for many a joke had he;
Full well the busy whisper, circling round,
Convey'd the dismal tidings when he frown'd;
Yet he was kind, or if severe in aught,
The love he bore for learning was in fault;
The village all declar'd how much he knew,

'Twas certain he could write, and cipher too;
Lands he could measure, terms and tides presage;
And e'en the story ran that he could gauge;
In arguing too, the parson own'd his skill,
For e'en though vanquish'd, he could argue still,
While words of learned length and thund'ring sound
Amazed the gazing rustics rang'd around,
And still they gaz'd, and still the wonder grew,
That one small head could carry all he knew.

I would now confidently conclude from Oliver Gold-smith's lines, that at some point, he was an invisible student in our classroom. He so accurately described and captured the very essence of the schoolmaster we all knew so well. Several students were convinced Goldsmith specifically wrote and tailor-made "The Deserted Village" to succinctly describe and summarize the gifts and characteristics our own schoolmaster possessed. Even though he was despised by some and tolerated by others, the majority, I am sure, will look back one day and fondly remember him as a man and an educator who always did his very best even when he was heard to say many times as he taught the lesser intelligent students, "It's true, you can bring the horse to the water, but you can't make him drink." There were other occasions when some students were convinced he could not teach a cat how to drink milk!

In spite of each student's perception of our schoolmaster, we all survived our schoolmaster days, moved on, and became solid citizens educated in the rudiments and skills necessary to lead a productive life. I'll let everyone speak for himself and share his or her individual experience of our schoolmaster, old "Yellow Bones." Personally, mine was truly positive and is fondly remembered. He was a perfectionist and a strict disciplinarian who did his best as he seamlessly taught third through eighth grades in one small classroom. He has long since gone to his eternal reward. Memories still linger on. He was instrumental in opening my mind to a lifelong love of poetry, learning, and intellectual curiosity, and yes, proverbs too. May his unselfish soul forever R.I.P.

Three

Life on the Farm

The Solitary Reaper

Behold her, single in the field,
Yon solitary Highland lass!
Reaping and singing by herself;
Stop here, or gently pass!
Alone she cuts and binds the grain,
And sings a melancholy strain;
O listen! for the vale profound
Is overflowing with the sound.
—William Wordsworth

Springtime on the farm in Ireland was both a busy and beautiful time. The heavy, woolen clothing worn during the cold winter was put aside and replaced with lighter, brightly colored dresses and skirts for the girls and short britches for the boys. My mother had been busy making the dresses over the long winter. The boys' long pants were pleasantly exchanged for short britches. Fresh, new green growth covered the grass, trees, and shrubs and a feeling of renewed life abounded everywhere. The birds sang in the trees as they busily gathered twigs and grasses to build their nests. The daffodils, in full bloom, bobbed their heads to and fro as if dancing.

The turnip crop, adjacent to our house, was an unkempt sight where weeds, growing aplenty, crowded and choked off young seedlings. The carrot and cabbage patches were overgrown too. It was for us children that dreaded time when we were charged with the chore of separating seedlings and pulling the weeds. This job awaited us just as soon as we ate our dinner when we came home from school. When we finished eating the meal, which my mother placed on a big, blue, willow-pattern platter in the center of the table, we changed from our school clothes into work clothing and then went outside to pull some weeds. We ate our meal family-style, often sharing the same plate with another sibling. We did not have enough everyday dinnerware for everyone, especially when we all ate in a group at the same time.

The "good china" was reserved for very special occasions like wakes, a visit from the priest, or when the station was at our house. Dinner in our house for the adult family members was usually served around one o'clock in the afternoon. It consisted of cabbage that was first boiled and then fried in bacon drippings to add extra flavor, ham or bacon, potatoes, and a hearty serving of fresh vegetables gathered from the garden that morning. Our meal was followed with a drink of milk to maintain our calcium intake level.

When my mother served the adults their meal she set our dinner aside and kept it heated in a cast iron pan by the fireside for us when we came home from school. The young, green cabbages and the fresh carrots pulled from the garden that morning were served on a regular basis and were always a treat. My granduncle planted a vegetable garden in the spring. We were fortunate to have a supply of fresh peas, carrots, parsnips, cabbage, beets, onions, and turnips available throughout the year. Even though some of the vegetables were seasonal, we could usually count on having enough cabbage, carrots, and turnips, to last through the winter.

In wintertime, when I came home from school, my mother often served a hefty helping of either stew or thick vegetable soup made from the beef bones that she had simmering by the fireside for hours. As she encouraged us to eat a good meal, she would say, "That will stick to your ribs and keep body and soul together." The hot, tasty, thick soup sated and warmed me up quickly and then I would be ready to work on the waiting projects and chores.

Pulling weeds seemed to get the highest priority and it was the one chore I disliked most. After weeding for a short while, my hands became irritated and smelled like the weeds themselves. The sap that leaked out as I pulled them was absorbed into my hands, turning them green, stinky, and slippery. The worst offenders were dockin leaves, thistles, buchalauns, crawdawns, nettles, dandelions, and crab grass. Red shanks and chickweeds were easier to pull because their roots were close to the surface. Some weeds had a generous supply of sap and prickly thorns, particularly dandelions and thistles. The deep rooted dandelions had an abundance of milk-like sap that squirted all over my clothing when the stems broke. They grew fastest, and had the deepest roots. While grasping the stem to remove the plant, I had to get the entire root out so the weed would not grow again.

Following the completion of the weeding job, I worked at thinning out the turnip crop. This was a monotonous job because our granduncle stood aside and watched while urging me to move faster and faster with the promise of a treat when the spring jobs were finished. The purpose of thinning turnips was to expand the crop and obtain a more abundant yield. Turnips were sown from seed, which grew in bunches in some areas and sparsely in others. So, for a uniform crop, thinning and transplanting was the solution. This process expanded the size of the crop from a mere little patch into a larger area. While handling the young turnip seedlings, I was careful not to break the stems, which would render them useless for transplanting.

Now that the weeding and thinning the turnips jobs were completed, I undertook the arduous job of picking stones in a bucket from the fields and stashing them neatly in piles until they were collected by the County Council workers who used them for local road repair. Picking stones was most unkind to my young, tender hands. The rough-edged stones often grazed my finger-tips and scratched the palms of my hands. After that, no job was difficult for a young farmer's daughter. To prevent infection, and at my mother's urging, I washed my hands in a solution of warm water laced with Jeyes Fluid, a strong, all-purpose, household disinfectant.

When the fields were plowed and ready for the potato crop to be sown, neighbors asked us children to lend a helping hand guggering, the process of dropping splits the woman of the house had been cutting from seed potatoes. It was a wonderful opportunity for me to earn a few shillings for myself. Since we were the only family for miles around with several children, neighbors booked us well in advance to gugger. During the evening, after teatime, when my mother finished milking the cows and completed her usual daily chores, she sat down, armed with her little sharp knife, and cut the seed potatoes into splits. She was an expert at cutting them, fast and accurate with her knife. Each potato produced at least three or four splits depending on the number of eyes or buds it had. My mother made sure each split has at least two eyes to insure growth. She knew a split with two eyes had double the odds of taking root than those with only one eye. Splits were sown in the prepared ground usually within 48 hours of cutting. If they were left unsown for a longer period, they would shrivel up and dry out, rendering them useless.

The bags of splits were transported to the potato field by ass and cart. A bag of freshly cut splits was placed at the top of every fourth or fifth ridge, from which the guggerer filled his bucket then dropped them one by one into holes the potato setter had made with his skeeveen, which was a long, wooden tool made from the handle of a spade, shovel, or pitch fork. One end was tapered to a point, similar to an extra-large pencil. On one side, and about six inches from the pointed end, was a pedal, which the setter pressed down on with his foot to make the holes for the guggerer to drop the splits into. It was important to have all the splits cut uniformly as the skeeveen was nonadjustable and could not accommodate splits that were bigger than the holes.

When the planting season chores were accomplished, it was time to proceed to the peat bog where cutting turf was already underway. It was the children's job to spread the turf out to dry. This, too, was another chore that was hard on the hands. The little twigs in the rough, heavy, wet peat often got embedded into my hands like splinters. Under a fingernail was the most painful place of all to get one. Should that be your misfortune, trying to get it out was even a painful ordeal. If it did not come out by using hot soaks, it meant the victim needed to get the cure of the thorn made. Splinters qualified as thorns and the cure of the thorn, a homemade remedy, was the most likely solution to extricate them.

One of my most vivid childhood memories during the summer is when a neighbor's son-in-law, his wife and children, while on vacation, came to our house on a Sunday afternoon to visit my parents and greet us children. They lived in Dublin and rarely came to our part of the country, so for us this was a big event that warranted entertainment in the parlor. Fortunately, they came on a Sunday afternoon. It was the practice in our area to remain dressed in our Sunday best the entire day as a show of respect for the Lord's Day. This visiting gentleman had a camera dangling from a long black strap around his neck. It was a beautiful, sunny day and he invited my entire family outdoors to pose for a group photograph. Indoor photography was not yet an option for the casual photographer in those days. My parents were thrilled at his offer because they did not have a photograph of our entire family. Preparation and coordination were major undertakings as the photographer tried to get my parents and ten children, six girls and four boys (another boy would arrive three years later), ranging in age from six months to seventeen years to line up, by age and height order, and watch the birdie.

My younger siblings and I were looking all around for a birdie, never before having seen a camera. We had no idea what this new gizmo was all about or how it worked. To us children, a birdie was a scaldie, a young, helpless baby bird not yet capable of flying. We all wondered how he could see a birdie and we couldn't, so we tried all the harder to spot this elusive birdie. The photographer, after much shuffling and side-stepping, took a step forward, followed by a half-step backward, all the time looking quizzically down at the camera, which he held about waist high, with one hand arched over its top to shield the lens from the sunlight, and began to focus and capture the entire group within the outline of the frame. When all the focusing and side-stepping were accomplished, he asked that we not move from our rigid statue-like positions. His next command to all of us was to say Cheeeeese. At that point, he swayed backward a little then pushed a button and with a click the job was finished.

To my parents' great surprise, several weeks later they received an envelope in the mail with the name and return address of the photographer clearly written on the flap. Upon opening it, my mother discovered it contained a wonderful photograph of our large, happy family filled with good posture and broad grins. We treasured and still treasure that picture; the only one ever taken of us when we were young children. From time to time, I look at that time-worn, now old photograph, and cheerfully reflect on all the primping and preening, stopping and starting, that magically went into its creation that day, long ago, when we all obediently kept our eye on the birdie, now frozen in time.

Toward the end of August when the outdoor chores were completed and a new school year had not yet started, my granduncle treated us to an afternoon at Duffy's or Fosett's circus, whichever one was in town that particular season. This was the long-awaited day we looked forward to very much. It was his annual reward for our hard work over the spring and summer months. The circus was held on the Fair Green, under a tent, in the center of our local village. Even though the performance did not start until three o'clock in the afternoon, we were up at the crack of dawn and ready to go see it by ten o'clock in the morning. The excitement and anticipation we experienced were beyond description. Our granduncle yoked up the donkey and cart in preparation for the trip to the circus. The younger ones sat in the body of the cart and he sat on a wooden board that crossed from side to side so he could easily drive the donkey and keep his eyes both on the road and on us.

Our house was situated approximately four and one-half miles distant from our local town. The trip to the circus took a little over an hour. During the performance we saw sights and feats we had never seen before. Dogs jumped through hoops, from chair to chair, walked on their hind legs, and amazingly went up and down ladders without missing a step. Horses trotted around in a circle with young women riders jumping from the back of one horse onto the back of another without slipping and falling off. Three men and two girls did a high wire act, to the beat of loud music, as they swung freely and exchanged places on a small platform high above the ground. We were totally fascinated by all the action and, at the same time, we were scared to look for fear one of them would miss their target and come crashing to the floor. Two or three clowns ambled around on stilts, entertained the children, and gave out candy while others rode unicycles or engaged in other antics. All in all, the entire performance lasted about an hour. To us children, that was a piece of priceless entertainment that left a lasting impression on my mind.

Going to the circus indicated the summer holidays were almost over and the return to the classroom was fast approaching. For months following the circus, we talked about it among ourselves and shared our experience and excitement with our classmates when we returned to school. Just as soon as we were faced with the routine of learning and study, we put our fond memories of summer holidays and the circus aside and devoted our energy and attention to our lessons.

As autumn closed in and while we were in school, my father and granduncle were out in the potato field digging the potatoes. Again, when we got home from school we were assigned the job of potato picking. This was a two-part job consisting of picking the large potatoes first and leaving the smaller ones behind for another child to pick. Some of the big potatoes were stored in a heap at the end of the field, which was covered with straw and rushes topped off with an outer layer of soil to prevent freezing during the winter months. The remaining potatoes were brought into the barn for household use. The smallest ones were set aside in a separate area to be used as feed for pigs, hens, and turkeys.

As the autumn season moved onward and the days got shorter, our thoughts turned to Halloween. This was a time for lots of excitement. My father had little tolerance for what he considered idle amusement. The schoolmaster told us about ducking for apples, barm bracks, and other Halloween traditions. Barm brack was a round raisin loaf made only at Halloween that contained a fake ring. It was said that the person who found the ring would be married before the next Halloween. No doubt, another folklore tale, but an exciting one, especially if there were children of marriageable age in the house.

We were more fortunate than other school children because we passed a grove of apple trees on our way to and from school. Oftentimes, we wandered among them to snatch a few apples, which we carefully stowed away until Halloween. On that day of fun and games we placed a few apples in a basin of water and ducked for them. My father associated Halloween with paganism and witch-craft, so when we engaged in this apple-ducking activity

51

we did so when he was not around. It was with fear and excitement that we did our ducking. On one hand, we were scared that some kind of pagan curse might befall us while, on the other, we didn't want our classmates to know that we did not engage in similar activities to them.

Following Halloween, it was our usual custom to go to confession in preparation for Mass on the feast of All Saints followed the next day by the feast of All Souls. The month of November was set aside to pray for the dead and particularly for the dearly departed souls in Purgatory who had no one to pray for them.

In our house, every night we gathered around the fireside, on our knees, and prayed the rosary. My father was the leader, saying the introductory prayers and the first decade. My mother said the second. My grandmother said the third, my granduncle the fourth, and my oldest brother the fifth. Following the Hail Holy Queen, my father started the trimmings. He offered one Our Father and three Hail Marys for the well-being of our family. My oldest sister would say them. As he offered additional petitions, those responses were intoned by those of us children who knew our prayers and so on until everyone got a turn. The trimmings of the rosary took longer to complete than the five decades.

By the time my father had included everyone and everything he wanted to pray for, my grandmother started with incantations for her daughters in America, the sailors on the high seas, and the dearly departed who had no one to pray for them. And so the list went on and on. Oftentimes she repeated herself and prayed Hail Marys and Holy Marys over and over for the same intentions. One Our Father and three Hail Marys often became two or three Our Fathers and five or six Hail Marys. Then for good measure, she would start the

Litany. Every saint that was ever canonized, and some that were not saints at all, were called upon to intercede for all kinds of intentions. Praying the rosary in our house took at least an hour and oftentimes more. Our knees were sore and full of indentations from kneeling for a long period on the rough, concrete floor. If a neighbor came to the door while the rosary was in progress, he automatically dropped to his knees and joined in. The rosary was not interrupted for any reason whatsoever. We often gave a sigh of relief when it was finally finished.

Following the rosary, some neighbors came by for a ceili, an informal social visit. One man, in particular, entertained us with ghost stories. Many of them were so real and so scary that we were afraid to go upstairs to bed. His stories usually evolved around graveyard settings, someone recently deceased or a very ill person close to death. He told us about the banshees he had seen and heard wailing around houses for either departed or soon to be departed souls. He often put the hair standing on our head with his tales about the lights, of unknown origin, that illuminated the homes of those close to death and the wandering spirits he had encountered while outside after dark. He had the capacity to embellish his stories and relate them with such conviction that we shook with fear and yet we listened attentively to be sure we didn't miss a detail. On many occasions, when we went to bed, we arose shortly thereafter and looked out the bedroom window, half scared, but still hoping to see a ghost, a banshee, or some strange lights and share our experiences with the neighbor, the storyteller. Whether real or imaginary, there were several occasions when we saw strange lights bouncing around in the distance. It was customary to believe that when mysterious, unexplained lights or banshees were seen in close proximity to a house, someone in that house had either recently died or would soon die.

One of my most vivid recollections is a particular ghost story my father told about an experience he had on his way home from town after dark. While riding his bicycle along a winding lane, something very strange happened. As he was pedaling along, a powerful, invisible force stopped his bicycle and he was thrown to the ground. He arose and got back on his bicycle again. Just as soon as he started to pedal off, the same force stuck his bicycle to the ground and he could not move it. He broke out in a cold sweat, reached into his pocket and pulled out his rosary beads. He said a decade of the rosary and with that his bicycle took off by itself. He ran after it, jumped on, and pedaled home as fast as he could. From that day onward, he always carried his rosary beads on his person.

On another occasion, when my brother and three of his friends were cycling home from a dance, they passed a coffin being carried by six men all dressed in black. They thought it most unusual to see such a sight at two o'clock in the morning. It was the custom in our area not to pass a funeral; instead, you stopped in your tracks and waited for the funeral to pass you. Since this was the tradition, my brother and his friends got off their bicycles, pulled over to the side of the road and waited for the funeral to pass them. They waited long enough for it to have reached them, but instead of a funeral passing, the only thing that passed by was a small black dog. That experience had such a profound effect on one of them that he was taken to the hospital suffering from fright and confusion. Another was left speechless for several days and none of them ever traveled that road again after dark.

There were many ghost stories, personal experiences with ghosts, and other scary tales and events discussed that we never knew if they were real or imaginary. That was left to one's own imagination. The existence or non-existence of ghosts was considered a supernatural experience and was not questioned or challenged. Our strong Catholic upbringing and deep sense of faith were so well ingrained in us that we would not question or doubt experiences that could not be rationally explained.

Two of my greatest fears as a child were water and lightning. Just as soon as my mother saw the first flash of lightning, she broke out the holy water and sprinkled it around the house and on us children. She gave fair warning to be sure to bless ourselves and say an Act of Contrition in case one of us might be struck or killed by a lightning bolt. When she finished sprinkling, she immediately got a bed sheet or a tablecloth and covered up the sideboard mirror in the parlor. That was the only mirror in our house that was called a mirror; the one my father used while shaving was called a looking glass. She covered the looking glass with a towel so it, too, would not attract or reflect lightning. It was her belief that mirrors reflected lightning and by covering them there was no danger of it striking anything else. She was a remarkable protector of her family.

We did not go near any body of water except on those occasions when we were in the bog saving turf or watching the neighboring men fishing in the river a short distance away. My mother had warned from me from early on never to stare directly at water because doing so would cause a reeling in my head, make me stumble or keel over and fall in. Whenever I was by the river I sat on its bank and watched the fish swim to and fro. I knew the moment I started to feel dizzy it was time to drop backwards to quickly recover from the reeling state. This was a summertime concern for my mother, who was always comfortable when we were either within her line of vision or the sound of her voice. Since we spent more time outdoors and she was busy inside the house with my grandmother and small children, she could not abandon them to oversee what we were up to. Possibly, it may have been nothing more than a threat on her part to be sure we would not engage in reckless behavior or silliness near or around water. Whatever her motive was, it worked well and taught us a lifelong respect for water. The older I get, the smarter and more caring my mother seems to get, even though I have no particular intention of putting into practice many of the lessons she taught and examples she used. Even though I was very close to her, I don't remember her demonstrating any open manifestation of affection. Like most Irish mothers in that era, she kept her feelings locked up in her heart. My emotions and feelings are much more open and spontaneous—due, I'm sure, to my lifestyle and exposure to diverse cultures in the United States of America.

As winter drew closer, we looked forward to Christmas with great expectation and excitement. Our house was decorated with holly branches arranged on top of the dresser, the mantle, and windowsills. Of course, my mother wanted holly with plenty of red berries. Her penchant for adding color was evident. Since I was a fearless and agile tree climber, I was designated to climb to the top of the holly tree, to collect the berried holly. Berries did not grow on the lower branches due to the lack of sunlight.

About a week before Christmas, and when our own house was decorated, my mother allowed my older sister and me to walk to town to see the decorations and the fairy lights that magically blinked in the shop windows. We did not have the luxury of having a Christmas tree or fairy lights in our house. They were considered a distraction from the true meaning of Christmas. It was not necessarily a matter of choice because we did not have any way of lighting them since electricity, in rural Ireland, was not yet available. It did not come about until several years later.

However, we enjoyed looking in the shop windows at the little twinkling lights the likes of which we had never seen before. In the middle of one shop window was a furry Santa Claus, about a foot tall, who rocked back and forth. For us, this was truly magical and it was the only time we had the opportunity to actually see what Santa Claus looked like. We had heard plenty of good stories about him. Even though we never saw his picture, we knew he would bring us some special treats for Christmas—that's what Mom and Dad told us.

Our Christmas preparation began on Christmas Eve when we walked to church for confession so we were in the state of grace to receive Jesus at Mass on Christmas morning. There were always long lines waiting outside the confession box. While we waited our turn to go into the confessional, fear would strike us in case the priest might raise his voice at some sin we confessed. I remember watching the older folks propping themselves up against the church wall and shifting their weight from side to side when someone inside the confessional took, what they considered, a very long time. They whispered under their breath among themselves remarking about the length of time such and such a person took in the confessional. They wondered what took so long and suspected the penitent must surely have a very long list of serious offenses to confess.

As soon as darkness fell on Christmas Eve, we placed lighted candles in the windows of our house. When it was dark, we went outside to admire their glow and enjoy the effect. While outside, we looked off in the distance at other houses to see if they, too, had put lighted candles in their windows. Houses with lighted candles stood out against the dark sky in stark contrast to the usually dark, cold Christmas Eve. The door to our house was left open all night as a gesture of welcome for wanderers and to let Mary and Joseph know there was room for them inside.

On Christmas morning we arose early and made a dash for the line of socks that hung from the mantle above the fireplace. We usually got a big, juicy Jaffa orange, a Peggy's Leg (a long, colorful candy cane), and a generous helping of conversation sweets with their little messages of love etched into them. Perhaps this was our parents' unspoken way of demonstrating their deep love for their children. We carefully separated the orange into sections and savored its refreshing juice. The candy we devoured in a flash.

Mass on Christmas Day was both sacred and special because the crib was set up with the Babe lying on the straw surrounded by Mary and Joseph, the ox, the ass, and a lamb. We learned in school each time we prayed before the Baby Jesus in the manger we would gain indulgences. These were a great way to reduce your stay in Purgatory, which is similar to Hell except it does not last forever. Our children's edition prayer book and prayer cards had a little note following the prayer indicating the amount of time you would get off your Purgatory sentence if you said that particular prayer. The goal was to say enough prayers to avoid Purgatory altogether and I quickly mastered the most advantageous prayers. Of course, it was also helpful to have a reasonably good mastery of math when adding up the days and years earned. Earning a plenary indulgence would eliminate Purgatory altogether. This was a very consoling thought, to avoid Purgatory and go directly to Heaven. The question always arose as to how many indulgences were enough. We had no way of measuring the rate of exchange. It was better to avoid sin altogether and concentrate on redemption, no matter how difficult the task.

Immediately to the right of the manger was a box with a slit in the top where donations in honor of the Babe in the manger were inserted. The sound of the coins as the donors dropped them in echoed throughout the church. On one occasion when my mother finished saying her prayers before the manger she made her donation. She took a coin from her pocket and dropped it into the collection box. On her way home from church, she stopped at the local shop to buy some treats for us children. When she reached into her pocket to pay her bill, she discovered the only coins she had were of small denominations. It was then she realized that she had unwittingly put the most valuable coin, a half-crown, into the collection box.

Embarrassed by what she had done in making such a generous donation, she feared she did not have enough money to pay for her purchases. She made the sacrifice of giving more than she could afford and she firmly believed we would be blessed in return for her generosity. Luckily, she realized she was wearing her heavy, winter coat, in which she usually kept some extra cash for emergencies, which she used to pay her bill. She often reminded us that whenever we gave beyond our means to the church, we would get it back one-hundred-fold in other ways—ways no amount of money could buy. Invariably she was right.

Mom's entire life revolved around family, caring for her children, church, attending to household duties and maintenance. Nothing was too much for her. Although nondemonstrative in her affection for others, she was a gentle and humble person filled with love and compassion who gave beyond her means without the slightest hint of expecting anything in return. It surely took a very special person to live under the same roof as her uncle and mother-in-law. However easy or difficult, she prevailed.

She had no time for those who engaged in boasting or bragging. It was because God filled her with so much of His love that she generously passed it on to us, her children. She was our consolation in times of sorrow, our hope during periods of doubt, and our strength in moments of weakness. Today, we struggle to live out those Christlike values and virtues she and Dad exemplified daily and taught us so well. We are all grateful for the gift of model parents.

A short while after Christmas, my mother read in the newspaper that the price of eggs was going up and she anticipated that if the hens laid eggs every day she would have recouped her unwitting donation to the Crib in no time. She was grateful to the neighboring woman who had swapped eggs with her earlier that spring. Instead of my mother's usual white Wyandotte chicks, usually unreliable egg layers, she now had a dozen young Rhode Island Red Pullets who faithfully laid big brown eggs everyday. The egg money was the spending money my mother used to buy herself a new hat or other personal items and always a special treat for us children. She enjoyed having a few shillings of her own to spend as she chose. Yet her greatness lay not in money, nor in power, not even in terms of education; rather, it lay in the gentleness, humility, and great love which anybody who knew her always experienced by her presence. In these chaotic times of the 21st century, I thank my mother and my father for their golden example. Their gifts, while not of worldly goods, were riches of true, unselfish, everlasting love.

In our area, a man with a van went from house to house every week buying eggs. It was a convenient service, but the price he paid was less than the going rate offered by the shopkeepers in town. He in turn sold the eggs he had bought from the local farmers' wives to a distributor for a much higher price. He was happy and the farmers' wives were happy for the convenience of the eggman. Selling eggs to the man with the van became routine. It was my job to collect the eggs from the hen house when I came home from school. I cleaned them before they were sold, being very careful not to break any. If I broke eggs in the process, that would cut down on my mother's pocket money and ultimately I would be the loser, especially if I was looking forward to getting new socks or material for a new dress.

On Christmas Eve, my mother looked over the chickens when she fed them. At a moment's notice she snatched up the plumpest among them and returned it to the hen house. That one would appear roasted and stuffed for dinner on Christmas Day. She made sure the chicken was fasting for at least twelve hours before it was killed. How I enjoyed a meal of roast chicken with all the trimmings. When the choicest pieces were distributed among the family, my mother, God rest her soul, usually served herself last. It was not unusual for her to put herself last.

On St. Stephen's Day, mummers visited every house in the neighborhood to amuse and entertain the occupants. They wore straw hats and had straw ropes tied around the bottom of their pants, Their faces were smeared with black shoe polish to disguise their appearances. One member of the group played an accordion, another played a fiddle, and another a tambourine or a flute. They were all excellent musicians. While they played Irish dance music the other members of the group took the floor and danced a half set around the kitchen, inviting the reluctant woman of the house to join in as well as any girls old enough to dance. It was customary to give the mummers a donation, for their entertainment. The money they collected was used to purchase a quarter barrel of Guinness for a spree (social gathering) held at one of the neighboring houses during the twelve days of Christmas. The spree was great fun and much enjoyed after the Advent season, when entertainment and dancing were forbidden.

In our house, each child had his own job assignment to work on after school. My oldest brother worked on the farm with my father. My oldest sister helped my mother with the laundry and baking, and the younger siblings with their homework. Our house did not have electricity, indoor plumbing, central heating, or running water. Homework was finished before darkness fell. We had a paraffin oil lamp that hung from a bracket attached to the window frame over the kitchen table. When that became outdated, it was replaced with a Tilley lamp—the forerunner to electric light.

Our large, country kitchen served as kitchen, dining room, and living room. It was there we spent our time when indoors, praying, chatting, laughing, sharing stories, and reading books and newspapers. During the long winter nights my father sat under the Tilley lamp to resole and cobble worn out boots and shoes. He needed bright light to see where to set the brads and trim the leather to a perfect fit. When he wasn't working on some project, he would break into storytelling. He often related stories about his own childhood and school days. Even though he had to drop out of school at age 12 following the death of his father, he was very smart and wise to the ways of the world. He especially enjoyed talking about world geography, the building of the Suez Canal, and the effect the war years, when goods were tightly rationed, had had on survival in Ireland. He was a forward-looking man knowledgeable in many topics, particularly agriculture, livestock, and farming. His goal was to get the best yield from crops. His fear was failure of a good return. A good oats crop meant more oats to take to the mill for grinding into oatmeal—another source of food for the family. Our home environment was such that it would never occur to any of us to disappoint our parents because they both worked hard. We showed our appreciation of their hard work by doing our very best to make them proud. That was the best—making parents proud of their children and their accomplishments.

At six o'clock every evening we listened to the Angelus followed by the six-thirty news on our battery-operated radio. Another program called Farmers' Forum, narrated by Michael Dillon, the radio voice of the farmer, was a nightly ritual. Local farmers, who did not have a radio of their own, came to our house several evenings a week to listen to the latest news and current events. When the battery charge was used up, one or two of us children carried it to town for recharging. The battery was filled with clear liquid, which we were told was some kind of acid, and we needed to be very careful not to spill any it as it would burn down to the bone. Needless to say, by the time we got to town, over four miles away, our hands were sore and tired from carrying the battery while holding it in a stationary position to avoid spillage.

It was a happy time in our house when the radio was working. Neighbors, on their way to our spring well, stopped in to hear the latest news and share tidbits of their own. Since we were the only family in the area that had constant supply of spring water on our property, we had visitors on a regular basis. When someone came to the door, my mother and father invited them inside and, as if by magic, a pot of tea was served up. My parents extended a hearty *cead míle fáilte* (a hundred thousand welcomes) to everyone and anyone who came by. Their great faith in God, warm hospitality, and love of visitors were the foundations for their unfailing generosity and kindness.

Our ever-faithful spring well was about one hundred yards from the scullery. As children, we were warned to keep away from it for fear one of us would fall in and drown since it was always full to the brim with clear, cold spring water. God forbid, a small child should fall in that would be catastrophic because a child's cry for help was beyond the earshot of my mother, who spent much of her time in the kitchen. The well was roughly four feet deep and five to six feet long, surely a source for certain drowning to an innocent, unsuspecting child should he or she have the grave misfortune to fall in.

Immediately beyond the spring well, was a grove of tall trees that we often climbed, in our spare time, until we reached the highest point to view the panoramic countryside all around. We each had our own favorite tree for climbing. Oftentimes, we got plenty of scratches and scrapes when we slipped off a branch as we moved up and down. Rarely, if ever, did we complain or discuss our injuries because my parents forbade us from climbing trees. We knew if we explained to our mother how we got all scratched, she would sternly reprimand us on the danger of the adventure we were engaging in. So, to avoid any additional punishment or reprimand, we quietly and discreetly bandaged up our wounds, behind her back, while we stoically endured the pain.

Four

Growing Up

Singing Bird

I have seen the lark soar high at morn,
Heard his song up in the blue,
I have heard the blackbird pipe his notes,
The thrush and the linnet too.
—Irish Melodies

The merry month of May, on the farm in Ireland, was a beautiful month to enjoy the great outdoors. The bleakness and rigors of winter were quite distant and it was easy to forget its dark, dreary days. Under an azure sky, bright, sunny days were upon us. New time was in effect, which gave us an additional hour of daylight for work and play. The song of the lark and the call of the cuckoo drifted all around the lush, verdant pastures. The curlew and the corncrake were busy seeking out suitable locations to build their nests. Nature had awakened from its long winter slumber and renewed life and growth were evident everywhere.

On these warmer days, I frequently tallied with my classmates on my way home from school, playing games, picking wild strawberries, blackberries and gooseberries, making daisy chains, and practicing my acrobatic movements, which I had seen performed in the circus, atop the stone bridge that spanned the river we crossed over every day. Indeed, we often detoured if there was a bird's nest or a new ass foal to be looked at and admired.

Along the way, we listened to the sound of the blacksmith's hammer emanating from the forge nearby as he clanged on the anvil while he bent and shaped horseshoes and ass-shoes, plough parts, iron gates, as well as a variety of farm implements brought in by the local farmers for either repair or replacement. We hoped he would give us a chance to strike the anvil to hear who made the loudest noise. The forge was an exciting place to watch the large bellows send the sparks from the coal fire flying in all directions.

Under a spreading chestnut tree
The village smithy stands;
The smith, a mighty man is he,
With large and sinewy hands;
And the muscles of his brawny arms
Are strong as iron hands.
—"The Village Blacksmith,"
by Henry Wadsworth Longfellow

The sound of the bellows and the swish of the hot metal as he cooled it in a water trough still linger in my ears. Our local blacksmith was a repository of all the local news and current events in the area. He shared news of weddings, births, illnesses, and deaths. He reported on horse and cattle fairs, telling the prices obtained and relaying the gossip, whispers, and rumors he had gleaned from those he came in contact with. Indeed, he was, in many instances, the storehouse of more news than the local newspaper. Invariably, on their way to and from town, the farmers stopped by the forge for a chat, to share stories, or rest awhile and watch him work as he skillfully molded the strips of iron into perfectly fitting horseshoes. Occasionally, a visitor would ask him to make a horseshoe to hang over their kitchen door as a good luck charm. It was said that the most powerful charm against bad luck was a horseshoe hanging over the entrance door never to be taken down or touched.

Our local blacksmith was a talented man, knowledgeable in cures, predictions, and weather conditions, widely known to warn sheep farmers that if the first lamb of the season was born black, it was a sign that the owner would be in mourning within the year. He could accurately tell the time of day by looking toward the location of the sun in the sky and predict the weather using a homemade weather gauge, which he made from a clear glass jar half-filled with water with an inverted bottle on top so that the rim of that bottle rested on the water. When the water moved up into the neck of the inverted bottle, it was an indication of a rising barometric pressure indicating favorable weather was in the forecast. If the water did not move, no change in conditions was imminent for the upcoming days.

Spring was the busiest season for both the blacksmith and the farmers. It was when they got their horses shod, their ploughs repaired, and made ready to prepare the soil for the planting and sowing season. Winter was the blacksmith's slowest season because the days were colder and visitors were less frequent, allowing him time to enjoy the sounds of nature echoing through the thatched roof and the broken window. He often spoke of how much he enjoyed the racket the crickets made around his coal fire. Crickets were looked upon as the luckiest inmates of a dwelling; anyone who killed a cricket, it was said, would incur the wrath of the cricket family who would assemble and eat up his clothes in retribution for the loss of a friend or relative.

Oftentimes, we children stopped by the forge to greet and sometimes tease the blacksmith. We never left without checking out the weather gauge for future weather predictions. Even though he was a kind man who was covered from head to foot with the black soot which arose from the residue of the hot metal when he cooled it in the water trough, he often threatened us with the frequent reprimand, "I'll tell your father next time I see him about your behavior." In our own ironic way, we both loved and feared him because if he did report us to our parents, likely we would be firmly chastised. The sounds from the forge are long since silent: no more blacksmith, no more anvil, no more socializing, no more familiar sounds and cheers from the assembled locals playing pitch and toss outside its door on Sunday afternoons. The horse and the ass have long since given way to the automobile. The farming equipment has been replaced by modern, state-of-the-art machinery and modem technology. Telephone conversations and electronic messages have replaced the one-to-one communication and shared stories. That little local hub of friendly activity exchange is replaced with electronic and mass media communication with their scant, impersonal reporting of national news and weather predictions so far removed from the intimate exchanges shared when neighbors and passersby gathered at the local forge.

Our Saturday chores included polishing several pairs of shoes for Mass on Sunday. Following Mass, we usually played the game of skittles. This game was, in one sense, the forerunner of what today we know as bowling. It was played with five short, round pieces of wood set up in a square—one piece at each of the four corners and one in the center. They were made from the handle of a spade or shovel that was cut into lengths of about six to eight inches. The object of the game was to knock down as many skittles as possible with a longer piece of wood called a thrower. The four corner pieces had a value of five points each and the one in the center had the high value of ten points. Each participant got two turns at throwing. The distance from the skittles to where the thrower stood was about fifteen feet—a little shorter if there were younger children playing. Should a player be fortunate enough to knock down all the skittles with one throw, he earned a bonus of five additional points. At the outset, it was agreed that the game would end when a player reached the total score of either the decided goal or, at the very most, one hundred points. It often took us over an hour to complete a game and reach either one hundred points or the decided upon score. Wild throws (either too short or too long), fooling around, or not concentrating on knocking down enough skittles to earn bonus points, which made the game move along faster, were the usual game delay factors.

As children, one of our favorite things during the month of May was gathering wild flowers and placing them in a vase, a tin can, or a jam jar in front of a statue of Mary. Of course, vases were seldom available and those that were around were usually stored safely away, well out of the reach of children. We often improvised empty bottles and used them as vases for our bouquets of flowers. May, being the month of Mary, and in her honor, we picked wild flowers and sprinkled them on the doorsteps of the houses we passed on our way to and from school. Occasionally, when we passed a house that had roses in bloom, we picked them, separated the petals and spread them on the doorsteps, too. One of the highlights of the month of May was the procession in town when a large statue of the Virgin Mary was carried aloft through the streets. It was preceded by schoolgirls, dressed in their white Holy Communion dresses, carrying small baskets filled with rose petals and wild flowers, which they dropped on the pavement ahead of the elevated statue. In our village, the final leg of the procession proceeded up the main street to the chapel that overlooked the town. When the statue reached the chapel and was set in its place, the priest led the congregation in prayer followed by a Holy Hour, singing of hymns, and closing with benediction. I recall wondering why the priest wrapped his decorative shawl around the base of the monstrance containing the Blessed Sacrament and suspected it must be hot and that was why he used the material to cover his hands and protect them from being burned.

One day, on my way home from school, I practiced dangling by my chin from atop the stone-wall bridge we crossed. While dangling fearlessly, I lost my grip and toppled down into the river below. I landed on my side and crashed into a large boulder, which I hit with such full body force that I almost fainted. Fortunately, the water in the river was quite low and I did not get too wet. Unfortunately, for me, however, it was not high enough to cushion my fall. When I finally got back on my feet, with help from my classmates, I soon realized something was terribly wrong with my left arm. Upon examination, I could see it was totally misshapen. My elbow was at the front instead of in its usual position at the back of my arm. With assistance, I was able to walk from the river bed onto dry land. Feeling dizzy and disoriented, I collapsed on the grassy ditch along the road. After a short while, I recovered well enough to walk slowly and cautiously until I finally reached home. When I entered our house, my mother looked at my arm, saying with tears streaming down her face, "Oh, my God, what will I do? It'll have to wait till your father comes home." My father was in town at a cattle fair and my mother knew nothing could be done for me until he came home. My oldest brother was about twelve, too young to get the horse from the field. My two older sisters were eleven and ten. I was next, and I was eight and a half. My younger siblings ranged in age from six to infancy. The telephone was not an option in our area. My very concerned mother had no possible way of reaching or communicating with my father at the fair. He was the only one who could fetch the horse to take me to the bonesetter. The greatest consolation my mother could offer was to place me in her own bed, away from the noise and activity of my younger siblings. That, to me, even then, was a true demonstration of her love and concern. Today, I ask myself, "Can you just imagine, a child with a broken arm waiting indefinitely before getting help?"

I well remember when the fair day was a big outing and special occasion for the neighbors and farmers who traveled many miles to renew acquaintances and discuss the events of the day. There was great excitement in our house the morning of the fair. My father and oldest brother arose early, assembling the animals to be sold so they were ready for the trip. Oftentimes, my father felt a hint of sadness if some animals were around for a long time and we had become attached to them. Before hitting the road, my mother would prepare a hearty breakfast, usually Boxty, which would carry them over until their next meal. Because of unpredictable weather, my father and brother dressed warmly and left early in the morning usually before daylight, making sure the animals were not rushed or tired from their walk, arriving at the fair around daybreak. Also, they wanted to secure a prominent position to show the animals. Many farmers had their favorite location and my father was no different. When they settled in they could relax and prepare for what they hoped would be a successful day.

My father enjoyed relating the tales about the fair and how cattle dealers (jobbers) came from across the border in the North as well as from other distant parts of the country. He often encountered them quite a distance ahead of the fair location. They were looking for bargains from the unsuspecting farmers who were taking their animals to the fair. The jobbers would look the cattle over, and often make sarcastic comments about them, oftentimes saying, "We'll take them off your hands and save you the bother of making the entire trip." My father was quite familiar with dealing with these boyos, making them soon realize he would not fall for their line and letting them know that there was nothing forthcoming. Then they would move on to annoy someone else and insult him with downgrading remarks about his livestock.

As the day progressed, the jobbers would patrol the street taking note of all the stock on show. When they saw an animal they were interested in, they conducted a closer examination, looking at the animal from side to side, poking and prodding and counting its teeth. Then, reluctantly, they would ask, "How much do you want?" When told, they would shake their head and drift away, but they would return because they liked to play a waiting game. When they returned, the more serious business of buying and selling would begin. It was customary for the seller to ask a higher price than he expected to get, and the buyer to offer a lower figure than he would pay, so the bargaining would start. Some of the comments used were, "When did you feed this animal last?" or "The poor thing, look at how the bones are sticking out; you're a lucky man it made it this far," and on and on, making offers matched by counter-offers. When I got older, I experienced these activities firsthand and my father had made no mistake when he quoted those hard-nosed cattle dealers.

When a price could not be agreed on, a third party often intervened asking, "What's between ye'z men?" On being told, he'd say "C'mon lads, split the difference and make it a deal." If both parties were still reluctant, he would grasp each man's hand and say, "Now, don't break my word." Then they would engage in a lengthy debate over the "Luck Penny" and the deal was completed with both men spitting on their right hand and slapping them together. The buyer would then put his mark on the animal's back for identification purposes, indicating the deal was closed and the animal was sold. Payment usually took place in the local pub where conversation recounted how a bargain was struck and deals were made. When the activity of the fair day was over, the business people would proceed to clean up the waste around and outside their premises. On the way home, it was not unusual to come upon animals that hadn't been sold seen rambling home alone; the owners might still be inside the pub not aware the fair was over, still engaging in the banter and the bargaining that had taken place several hours earlier as they slurped down another Guinness.

A popular feature of the fair, and one I enjoyed most, was the presence of stalls or stands on the street where vendors from outside the area sold clothes, footwear, household goods, cabbage plants, and produce. These traders, or "Cant Men" as they were called, usually advertised their wares by shouting loudly and proclaiming to have the best value in the fair. Again, the bargaining took place and many fairgoers oftentimes bought excellent quality clothing for their children at reduced prices. The fair offered an occasion for farmers to renew friendships and catch up on current prices and trends in livestock breed, usually followed by a stop in the pub for a drink and some well deserved socializing.

There was no estimating what time my father would be home to see what could be done about my misshapen arm. I remained in bed lying motionless until he came home. Upon his arrival, my mother immediately told him of my misfortune. He checked my arm and immediately realized I had to see the bonesetter. My mother bundled me up for the trip, gave me a hug, and whispered a prayer for my recovery. My father carried me down the stairs and together we set out in the horse and trap for the bonesetter's house. I have no recollection of either being afraid or being in pain. The bonesetter's house was approximately six or seven miles distant from our house. It took us over an hour to get there. She was an elderly woman, probably about seventy-five or eighty years old. Since I was a young child, she appeared really ancient to me. My father carried me in his arms from the trap into her kitchen. When I saw her, I became very frightened. She had no teeth and a deeply wrinkled face with white hair pulled back tightly and neatly arranged in a bun on top of her head. She was dressed in a hand-knitted black cardigan and a long black skirt that reached down to the top of her laced-up, high boots. I was eight years old at the time, and to me, seeing the way she was dressed and how she appeared reminded me of a witch. The only things missing were the broom and the tall, black, pointed hat.

While sitting in her kitchen, I suddenly became overcome by an involuntary trembling sensation. My knees were jerking and my entire body was shaking uncontrollably. The bonesetter asked my father to carry me outside in the fresh air, telling him that I would not be able to stand "the pulling" in my present condition. I did not understand what she was talking about and thought to myself, wondering what does she mean by "the pulling?" It was only when I was sitting outside in the cool evening air, on an upright, wooden kitchen chair, with her on my left side and my father on my right side, that it became evident to me what "the pulling" was. She sat facing me and held the wrist of my broken arm in her hand. Then, she asked my father to take hold of the upper part of my broken arm. Together they pulled until the separated bones snapped back into place. Ouch! The cringing of the bones as they shifted back together still lingers in my ears. The pain during this process was so excruciating that it caused me to temporarily lapse in and out of consciousness. The definition and my firsthand experience of "the pulling" is something I will never forget.

When the bones were back in place the bonesetter proceeded to make a cast from pitch, which she boiled in a little old black skillet over the open fire in the hearth. She then poured the thick, black liquid onto a piece of muslin, and while it was still very hot, she wrapped it around my broken arm. When that was done and the pitch was still soft, she bent my arm at the elbow to form the mold that would become the cast. As the pitch cooled down and set, it made a very strong, durable cast. Upon instruction from the bonesetter, I wore that cast for four weeks. When it was removed, the bonesetter made up another cast that she called a healing one. She made it from fresh soot, which she collected from her chimney in a well used, dented ponger (a tin cup) and added enough eggs to it to form a thick, gooey paste. When she was satisfied that the mixture had reached the right consistency, she poured it onto a piece of cloth roughly eighteen by ten inches. She let it settle for about fifteen minutes until it congealed. Lifting up this messy mixture, she wrapped it around my arm. This was the healing cast. She indicated the protein in the eggs, held together by the soot, would help my broken arm heal and once that cast came off, I would then need to get the cure made to limber my elbow. My most memorable recollection of the healing cast is the terribly offensive odor that came from it. On the plus side, it was much more soothing than the original cast made from boiling hot pitch.

When the soot and eggs cast was removed, my arm, having been in two casts for several weeks, was both stiff and atrophied and I was unable to straighten it out. At this point, I desperately needed the cure to limber and get it back to normal. It was a classic example of much needed physical therapy—again unheard of then. Fortunately, my father was able to locate a man, on the other side of town, who had the cure for limbering. That cure was a concoction of vinegar, alum, sugar-a-lead (I have no idea what that was), mentholated spirits, the roots of dandelions, comfrey, ginger, more herbs, and ingredients boiled together then strained and poured into a bottle for my father to take home. My mother applied this limbering mixture to my arm three or four times a day, saying the prayers assigned by the man who made the cure when she did so.

When the limbering cure mixture was completed, then the final stage of recuperation included a massage with goose grease two or three times a day. In our area, goose grease was difficult to find for a couple of reasons.

We did not live near water and, even if we owned geese, they would have no place to swim. Only farmers who lived near water and owned many geese could afford to kill one of them for dinner or a special occasion. It was a challenge for my father to find someone who had recently killed a goose and likely saved its grease. Since goose grease was a popular component of cures for several different ailments, there was a good possibility anyone who recently cooked a goose would save the grease for that purpose.

On his way home from church one Sunday, my father met up with a well-to-do Protestant family that lived by the lake and, sure enough, they had a gaggle of geese. He figured there was a good possibility they would have saved goose grease. And he was right. One day he went off on his bicycle to find these people and returned home several hours later with a small jar of the coveted goose grease. The Protestants in our area were much better off than the poorer Catholics. They had bigger farms, more and varied breeds of livestock and fowl, including geese, turkeys, bantams, and guinea hens. They owned the better land, and more of it, had larger homes, smaller families, and were always better dressed. After about two weeks of applying the goose grease to my arm it was truly miraculous how quickly its full range of motion returned. Hooray! An experience all too well remembered.

Our part of the country was noted for having a number of bonesetters and people with cures. They were much more popular than doctors and veterinarians. Invariably they were the first group to be consulted when a neighbor or member of our household had an accident or some strange malady. The most important thing about a cure was the person seeking it had to firmly and implicitly believe in its power and that it would work. One of our neighbors had the cure for ringworm. It was an ointment mixture made from unsalted butter, quick silver (mercury), and other secret ingredients known to him alone. The person in need of the cure would know some of the ingredients as he may be asked to bring them along in the event the cure maker did not have them on hand. The complete list of ingredients was a deep, dark secret not shared with anyone. The firm belief that it would work by the person seeking it was the most important requirement. As a rule, cures were secretly prepared behind closed doors where the ingredients were combined and the special prayers said. These prayers were intoned in a form of chanting, imploring the gods and supernatural powers to descend upon the cure and impart its power of healing to those suffering from the ailment in question.

Another nearby neighbor had the cure for a burn. It was a salve mixture that she made from unsalted butter and other secret elements. The patient would apply it to the affected area while saying the prescribed prayer. This process continued until the burn disappeared, usually within three or four days. The amazing thing about this cure was that when the burn healed, no scarring or discoloration of the skin could be seen. To cure a headache all that was needed was to tie a piece of a sheet that wrapped a corpse around the head of the sufferer and the headache would almost immediately disappear. Another popular cure for sore eyes was to mix clay taken from a holy well with fasting spittle and rub it on the eyelids then wait until the clay dried and wash it away. The sore eyes malady was washed away with the clay. One of the best remedies for an earache was to put some wool taken from a black sheep into the ear. Other commonly used cures and remedies were available for bleeding, cramps, sprains, warts, whittles, bloody noses, rheumatism, and on and on. There were few ailments or conditions that someone in our area did not make up a cure for.

The cure for whooping cough, jaundice, and worms was popular for children and was frequently sought ahead of medical attention. When the doctor made a house call, the condition was considered very serious and indicated the person needing medical attention must be close to death. It was invariably assumed that the priest, who would render the last rites, would soon follow the doctor. Not only were cures and customs a way of life, they were also very well respected and faithfully depended upon by the local populace for intervention and restoration.

If the cure for an ailment was sought, neighbors were not told. It was a secret privately shared between the person seeking the cure and the individual with the gift of making it. Whereas if the doctor was called to a neighbor's house everyone in the neighborhood could hear the sound of his car approaching. He was one of the very few that owned a car. Curiosity levels would peak until they found out who was so seriously sick. For the most part, people in our section of Leitrim were quite secretive and reluctant to share their personal business with anyone outside their family.

Cures were passed on from one generation to the next, usually from father to son, or mother to son. If there were no sons in the family, then they were passed to the oldest daughter. In every incidence, they were always passed to a direct bloodline descendant. Should there be no direct descendant, the cure vanished when its owner died. Cures were not only used for people disorders; farmers depended on their power of recovery when a disease or ailment struck their livestock.

In addition to cures, many local farmers firmly believed in superstitions and the power of patron saints and protectors. When the oats crop was sown, my father would place a pinch of blessed salt at the four corners of the field. This was said to ward off cutworm. When cutworm attacked the roots of the oats, the sprouts of the seedlings withered away and the crop failed.

Saint Anthony, the patron saint of lost articles, was always prayed to with the firm belief that he would lead those who sought his intercession to the site where the lost article was waiting to be found. Saint Lucy had the gift of healing eye problems. Saint Sebastian was prayed to for cranky children, and so the list went on and on with a patron saint for just about everything under the sun. Many times, if the particular patron saint was not known, another popular or more familiar saint was called upon to intercede and cure the problem.

Having had a broken arm and spending a long time in recovery, I was excused from partaking in outdoor work that entire summer. The rock-solid, cumbersome cast of pitch, which totally immobilized my arm, led me to fear there was a good possibility I would not be included with my siblings in our annual trip to the circus. As it happened, my granduncle had saved up the price of admission and treated all of us once again. I surely thought I would not be going this particular year as I had not done my share of work to earn the reward. I was delighted to be included in the annual treat of either Duffy's or Fossett's Circus, whichever one was coming to town.

They alternated each year to offer variety and hold the interest of the clientele. We were all mad with excitement when we reached town and made our way to the circus tent, which we could smell before we saw it. Before we took our seats, we stopped at the sweet shop and bought sweets to munch on during the performance. When buying sweets, we always looked for the best value for our money and invariably the ten-a-penny brand was what we chose.

I learned a lifelong lesson from my fall off the bridge. Instead of dangling precariously from it, I should keep my two feet firmly planted on the ground and never again practice what the acrobatic performers in the circus could do so well.

As summer rolled on, the golden meadows were now ripe for cutting. My father yoked up the horse and mowing machine and proceeded to cut the tall grass. The smell of the freshly cut grass was all around and it was a lovely aroma indeed. Once cut, it was left in swaths for a few days until some of the sap dried out before rearing it into the hay they used to fodder their cattle over the long winter months. Sometimes, even after a few days of drying, the grass was still wet due to occasional showers or heavy morning dew. In that case, we lapped the semi-dried grass in rows to dry out some more. Lapping was done by gathering and rolling the freshly cut grass into neat bundles that allowed the wind to blow through. This was a job for children and young people because their backs were more limber and flexible than their adult counterparts. Youngsters did not suffer from lumbago or back ailments often associated with the aging process.

Once the lapped hay had dried, it was ready to be put up in cocks. So that the top of the cocks would now blow away in the wind, a hay rope was made using an old-fashioned twister made from a length of wire, shaped like an S, with a hook on one end to grab the hay and a hand piece on the other for the twister to use while making the rope. Twisting hay ropes was a job usually reserved for the youngest person in the meadow or the person least helpful at saving the hay. When the rope was made it was placed across the top of the haycock and anchored securely at either side and then connected to a fistful of hay at the base. The stacked hay was left in the meadow until it was completely dry. Then it was drawn in to the hayshed where it was stored and used as fodder for the animals until spring.

The smell of the freshly cut grass was both refreshing and energizing. Watching the birds methodically filter through it and gather seeds for their young was fascinating. It was surprising to see how industriously and vigorously they combed through the dried blades of grass picking up wild berries and grass seeds and then carefully carrying their collection in their beaks back to their squawking young ones nesting in the nearby trees and hedges. Saving the hay was one of our more pleasant, outdoor summer jobs. The wonders of nature unfolded before our eyes. Regular visitors to a freshly cut meadow were the corncrake and the cuckoo. These rare birds seldom appeared at any other time of the year. Bringing the hay into the hayshed was a time for fun and games. As children, we played dress-up in skirts and headdresses made of hay. We romped, jumped, and rolled around in it, enjoying the soft, spongy feeling under our feet as well as the clean, fresh aroma of the clover and dried wild flowers that were generously mixed through it.

Working outdoors seemed to stimulate the appetite and it was with a sheer sense of pleasure and anticipation that we awaited tea time, when the warm five-naggin bottles or flagons of tea, securely wrapped in newspaper to prevent breakage, were brought out to the meadow in either a wicker basket, hand-woven by my granduncle, or a durable, double-handled shopping bag. There, inside the basket or bag were several mugs, the teapot filled to its brim with warm tea, sliced soda bread, generously buttered with the freshly churned, homemade butter, and sometimes my mother would surprise us and include "Boxty." No sooner was the tea poured into someone's mug than a big grasshopper would jump right into it. This was a problem that was easily and quickly solved. Once the grasshopper landed in the hot tea, he was either drowned or scalded to death. Then the floating carcass was picked out and tossed aside with a chuckle saying, "You won't do that again anytime soon."

"Boxty" and Colcannon were two dishes that were, I believe, unique to County Leitrim. "Boxty" is a tasty, very thin potato pancake, similar to a crêpe, traditionally native to Northern Ireland. Some of the neighboring farmers' wives adapted their own recipe to satisfy their individual taste. The standard recipe included: One pound peeled raw potatoes, salt and white pepper, one-half ounce of butter, one-quarter pint of milk, six ounces flour, one teaspoon baking powder and one egg, beaten. Cook half the potatoes in boiling, lightly salted water until tender. Grate the remaining potatoes into a bowl. Drain the cooked potatoes well, season with salt and pepper and mash with the butter. Mix the grated potatoes with just over half the milk, then beat in the mashed potatoes. Sift the flour and baking powder together, then combine with the potato mixture to form a soft dough. Mix the egg with the remaining milk and stir into the dough to form a soft, dropping consistency, adding extra milk if necessary. Drop spoonfuls of the mixture onto a heated, well greased griddle or thick-based frying pan and cook for three to four minutes on both sides or until golden brown. Serve hot with butter.

When I was very young, there was a popular rhyme about "Boxty": "Boxty in the griddle, Boxty in the pan; if you can't make Boxty, you'll never get a man." Every farmer's daughter aspired to excel at making "Boxty" for fear she become an old maid.

Colcannon, traditionally served at Halloween, often contained charms: a ring for marriage, a horseshoe for luck, a coin for riches, and a thimble or button for spinster or bachelorhood. It was originally made with kale, but more recently it usually contained cabbage. In our area the cabbage was omitted because of its pungent smell and bitter taste. The typical recipe ingredients include one pound of cabbage (optional) washed and shredded; one pound potatoes, peeled and cut into quarters; two leeks, trimmed and chopped; one-quarter pint milk or light cream; salt and pepper; a pinch of mace; and four ounces of butter, melted. The cabbage and potatoes were boiled in separate saucepans until cooked. Meanwhile, chop the leeks, add to the milk, and simmer together in a pan for five to ten minutes. Drain the cabbage and potatoes very well. Mash the potatoes, stir in the leeks and milk, and then add the shredded cabbage, seasoning, and mace. Combine very well, turn out into a deep serving dish, and heat through thoroughly in the oven, covering it with aluminum foil to prevent browning, if necessary. Make a well in the center of the mixture before serving and pour in the melted butter. Then sit back and enjoy!

When the hay was saved and brought into the haggard, it was time to concentrate on cutting the oats. My father started the cutting early in the day while we children were at school. When we came home, we went out to the oats field to tie the oats in sheaves. This was a process where the swath of oats was gathered into small bales and tied up with a belt made from a handful of straw. Toward the end of the day, the sheaves were gathered into groups of six or more and formed into stooks. They were left out in the field for a few weeks to dry and ripen. When the stooks were completely dry, the next step was to combine about eight or ten and stack them into a large handstack. After that, they were brought in to the haggard for threshing. This was a big day for farmers, second only to the Station. On threshing day, my father had a supply of burlap bags on hand to catch the threshed oats as they flowed from the threshing machine. Neighbors, once they heard the noisy sound of the thresher, automatically came to the house where it was set up to lend a hand. This gathering of helpers was called a "meithal." Oftentimes, as many as fifteen or twenty men would show up to help. Threshing was a synchronized process that included cutting the straw belts, feeding the sheaves into the threshing mill, and securely connecting the burlap sacks to catch the good crop at one side of the thresher. More sacks were connected at the other side to collect the second grade oats, and to avoid the danger or a backup in the engine, the chaff was kept clear of the mechanism.

Once the threshing operation started it could not be interrupted until every man simultaneously stopped working in his area of responsibility. That was usually done around one o'clock when the workmen shut down the limestone-fired engine and went to the kitchen, where my mother and older sister had dinner prepared and ready to serve. Those workmen had hearty appetites indeed. For the meal, a sizeable pot of potatoes, several heads of cabbage, and lots of boiled bacon were served and usually disappeared in quick fashion. When they finished eating their meal, they returned to their assigned jobs, finished up their assignments and then moved on to help with the next neighbor's threshing. The sense of neighbors helping neighbors was admirable and indeed the essence of a community that cared and shared. Having grown up in this kind of an outreach community, our lifelong values and respect for our fellow man were formed. Alas, with the advancement of modern technology, those days are gone by way of the turf fire and the mowing machine, replaced today by either central or solar heat or combine harvesters.

My generation is probably one of the last to have grown up prior to the introduction of electricity, the telephone, television, indoor plumbing, central heating, computers, telecommunications, frozen foods, cell phones, CD's, digital cameras, and fast food restaurants. Nowadays, these conveniences are the buzz words in many areas throughout rural Ireland. Today's young people are much more sophisticated, materialistic, and global in their perspective, as well as much more self-centered in their thinking. Their goals are self-motivated and not nearly as God-centered as they might be and were in times gone by. Even though I would not wish to return to many aspects of my life while growing up on the farm, I nevertheless learned respect for God's handiwork, loyalty to family and neighbors, as well as a less complicated and, at the same time, rewarding way of life. Today's younger generation never experienced those kinder, gentler ways their ancestors did in earlier days.

As we continue to look forward in this technological age of automation, globalization, and instant messaging, somewhere along our route we need to stop and ask ourselves, what price do we place on progress? How much have we given up in the process? What has happened to the fair days, the bonesetters, the cures, the fireside chats, and those warm personal greetings and exchanges we so looked forward to?

Five

Grandma: The Boss

The Death-bed

> We watch'd her breathing through the night,
> Her breathing soft and low,
> As in her breast the wave of life
> Kept heaving to and fro.
> —Thomas Hood

"Old Mam," as we grandchildren affectionately called her, was my father's mother and the only grandparent I knew. My maternal grandparents had died many years earlier. My mother's mother, and my godmother, died shortly after my christening. My maternal grandfather died several years before my mother and father were married. My paternal grandfather died when my father was a boy.

Since my father's father died when he was twelve years old, "Old Mam" assumed the role of both mother and father to him. I have no recollection of my father ever speaking of his own father and there were no pictures of him around the house that I ever saw. As a young man, my father was gregarious, warmly friendly, quick-witted on his feet, wise beyond his years, and astutely intelligent. He was quite handsome with steely gray eyes and black curly hair atop a lithe five-foot, seven-inch muscular body never weighing more than 10 stones (140 pounds) in his lifetime.

"Old Mam" was the surviving connection to my father's childhood and young adult life. Because she was a widow who had raised four children by herself, she was quite controlling and protective of him. She took care of her younger daughters and the household duties while my father worked the farm and tended the livestock. She depended on him and trusted him explicitly. The feeling was mutual. Their rapport was more like a partnership than a parent-child relationship. He had no solitary or private interests except to read the paper and from time to time to re-enter the house when he was working outdoors to check on his mother and share exchanges. He was the one who stayed behind when her daughters (his sisters) abandoned their homeland and immigrated to America as soon as they reached their teenage years.

When my mother and father married, "Old Mam" lived with them. Not only did she, but so did her bachelor brother, my granduncle, as well. She helped with running the household and raising us children as soon as we came along. She expected my father to shower her with the same attention he had given her across the years before he and my mother married. Adjusting to a daughter-in-law sharing the same kitchen and living space was not easy. As the saying goes, two women in the kitchen is one too many.

As a young woman, my grandmother spent a few years in America working as a nursemaid for a wealthy family in New York City. When she returned to Ireland, she brought back a large steamer trunk filled with linens, bedspreads, and delicately embroidered lace-trimmed bed covers and sheets. The intricate stitches and designs were all her own creation and would rival today's machine made, modern reproductions. These items remained locked up, smothered in camphor, in a trunk that sat on the landing at the top of the stairs in our house for as far back as I can remember. She reminded my parents on several occasions that it was her wish to have the sheets and bedspread used on her deathbed when she was laid out for reposing.

When she went to Mass on Sunday, she wore a black fur coat and matching hat that had an arrangement of colorful feathers swirling upward on one side. She brought these back from America too and took great pride in wearing them. The fur coat had deep pockets where she kept a supply of extra-strong peppermints and a few cloves in the event she got a bout of coughing during Mass. Cloves, placed on the tongue and allowed to slowly soften and dissolve, were the antidote used to suppress the desire to cough or clear the throat at inappropriate times, like during Mass, at a funeral, or in a crowded place where one did not want to call attention to oneself.

Her long, snow-white hair reached well below her waist. Each day she brushed it with a bristle brush, with its mother of pearl handle, and arranged it neatly in a bun, held together with ivory combs, on top of her head. The hairbrush and combs were also American products, mementos of her younger years in the U.S., the likes of which could not be found in rural Ireland in those days.

Around the house she was usually dressed in a long, black skirt over which she wore a full-length apron tied in a bow at the back. Her apron had a large pocket on the left-hand side where she kept her rosary beads and her old-age pension money. She kept the money tightly wrapped and tied up securely in a small, handmade purse with a drawstring running through the seam at the top, which she drew tightly and then knotted several times in case any of her pension money might fall out. She prayed the rosary every day for the well-being of everyone in our household and, in particular, for her three daughters in America, often muttering, "This decade is for Dolly, this one for Katie, and this one for Molly," as she broke into another round of her beads.

Although she was of slight build, she was hale and hardy, had a powerful grip, excellent eyesight, and a keen sense of humor. She did not participate in any chores around the house except to sweep the hearth from time to time on those occasions when she wasn't giving us children orders. She had a sharp memory and mind as well as acute hearing and was capable of threading a needle, reading the newspaper, and doing many intricate tasks, like sewing and darning, without the assistance of eye glasses. She and my father always remained tightly bonded, often reminiscing together by the fireside in the evening about past events and times gone by. They did this on a regular basis until she became bedridden shortly before she died, at the ripe old age of eighty-six years.

There were many occasions when she became very melancholy and wept after her three daughters in America, hoping one day they would return. As far as she was concerned, no one could ever take their place. She frequently and carefully scrutinized me and my sisters to see if we bore any resemblances to them, including the color and texture of our hair, color of our eyes, our level of intelligence, and other traits or characteristics she remembered her daughters, my aunts, having had. On many occasions she spoke of their intelligence and beauty. Our only regret was we children had never met them and regrettably we could neither agree nor disagree with her. We knew how much she missed them and how she loved receiving letters from them and we did our best to treat her lovingly and with the utmost respect.

Fortunately for me, I was named for her youngest daughter and I had inherited similar light brown, curly hair as well as being blessed with reasonable intelligence—qualities and characteristics she attributed to her. As a result, and to my good fortune, I was her favorite child. She often admonished one of my younger sisters who frequently dodged many near misses of the cámeen, the cane, my grandmother used to support her unsteady gait.

Before we went to school each morning, we took turns bringing tea and toast upstairs to "Old Mam," who usually stayed in bed until late morning, arising sometime after we left for school. She drank her tea from a china cup only, no substitute like a mug or tin cup was acceptable. As she advanced in her old age, her grip on the cup had become quite shaky, which caused her to occasionally spill the tea in her bed. When that happened, she called to my mother, who immediately changed the bed linens and proceeded to make her a fresh cup of tea.

My father was her only child who did not emigrate. He felt sorry for her continuous longing after his sisters in America and always tried his best to be kind and supportive of her. Even though his name was John, she called him "Sonny." That was the name he was known by his entire life.

My grandmother was very happy when she got a letter from any one of her daughters. She read it over and over again and then stuffed it down the front of her black cardigan next to her heart. Every once in awhile, when she thought no one was looking or noticed what she was doing, she would take the letter out and read it again and again. Awaiting the mailman was one of her daily routines. Invariably, she was hoping against hope for an envelope trimmed in red, white, and blue, indicating it came from the U.S., or the States, the name she called America.

Her three daughters wrote to her on a regular basis. Then, as time passed, her oldest daughter stopped writing altogether. I recall my grandmother being very worried and quite distracted because she had not heard from her in quite a long time. As time passed, "Old Mam" often paced the floor wringing her tightly clinched hands in front of her asking questions, of no one in particular, why her firstborn and oldest daughter had stopped writing.

One day, while my father was working in the fields, he got a letter from one of his other sisters with the news that their oldest sister had died. In the letter she warned him that he was not, under any circumstances, to upset their mother by telling her of the death. As the years passed, "Old Mam" would cry out saying, "Katie, I know you are with God. I only wish and pray someone would tell me for sure." Up until the time of her own death, she was never formally told that her oldest daughter had died in America more than twenty years earlier. Even though she had not been verbally told, she either instinctively or intuitively knew her eldest daughter was, in fact, dead. When saying the rosary at night, she prayed for the repose of her soul and begged God to show her His mercy.

Now that I reflect back on the pain my grandmother was enduring trying to handle the fear of the unknown, I truly regret the fact that her children did not tell her the real story. I am quite sure she would have accepted God's will and moved on. She went to her own grave without closure because of some silly reason for withholding the truth. Doing so did not lessen the worry and concern she was feeling. Even though she was spared hearing the sad news of having lost her child, her surviving children should have gathered together to share their loss. Whatever their reasons for the secrecy were, I will never know. Regrettably, that character flaw has bared its ugly head in my generation. An example being when my sister was hospitalized for brain surgery, my siblings in Ireland decided to spare my mother any anxiety and not tell her. I was already in America when that occurred almost twenty-five years ago. Trans-Atlantic communication with my mother was in letter writing. Of course, their intention was to tell her when the surgery was over and my sister was out of danger. Unfortunately, that was not the case. My sister died during surgery, and my mother, not knowing she was in the hospital, was shocked beyond words by the unexpected news. At that time, my father was already dead more than ten years. She did not have him, her partner as she called him, around to share her grief with.

When "Old Mam" reached her mid-eighties, she came downstairs less frequently. Rheumatism had crippled her joints and navigating the stairs became more and more difficult for her. While in her bedroom, she sat propped in bed with several pillows at her back and stared out the window for hours on end for no apparent reason that she ever made known. When she reached the stage that she was no longer interested in sitting up, she complained that her bed was always cold. My father purchased a hot water bottle to keep her feet warm. Her bedroom was quite large with a raised fireplace at one end. To maintain a comfortable temperature in the room, my parents lit a fire to keep her warm and cozy. That seemed to help and she settled down and appeared quite contented now that her feet were warm and the bedroom felt more comfortable. That bedroom was the warmest room in our house. It was located directly over the kitchen, which had a blazing fire continuously burning in the hearth during the day.

However, her comfortable feeling did not last too long. The sensation of being cold was beginning to overcome her whole body. She complained that her shoulders and arms felt cold. Extra blankets were put on her bed in the hope that they would help to keep her warm. In the midst of her throes of feeling cold, she was losing weight and becoming more crippled and incapacitated by the rheumatism that affected her joints and bones over the course of recent years.

Since I was her favorite child, my father designated me to sleep with her at night to help keep her warm. Of course, being of the young age of fourteen, I did not object to this sleeping arrangement. Each night I climbed into bed and cuddled up beside her. She often ran her gnarled fingers through my hair and told me of the great promise I held for her. Then together we said our prayers and she never went to sleep without saying:

Oh, Angel of God
My Guardian Dear
To Whom God's Love
Commits Me Here
Ever This Night
Be at My Side
To Light and Guard
To Rule and Guide
Amen.

This was one of her favorite prayers to our Guardian Angel. Once she had said it, she immediately followed up with another short one:

There are four corners on my bed
There are four angels at my head
Matthew, Mark, Luke, and John
God bless this bed that I lie on.

She was very happy she had taught me those prayers and, more importantly, that I could say them without any prompting. As soon as we said our prayers, she turned to me and said, "Now roll over and go to sleep." She usually slept a lot during the day and awakened at regular intervals during the night. While awake, she kept her eye on a small, luminous glow-in-the-dark statue of Our Blessed Mother, which sat on the mantle over the fireplace in her bedroom. The pale glow of the statue often made me feel uneasy as it eerily pierced the darkness of the room.

One cold day in early February, my parents decided I should no longer sleep with "Old Mam." I did not understand the reason for the change. As a matter of fact, my father moved the second bed from her bedroom, where my sisters slept, across the hall to my parents' spacious bedroom. Their room was a large, airy room that extended from one side of the house to the other with enough room for another double bed. At this point, "Old Mam" seemed to be talking less and less and sleeping more and more. She was losing her appetite and neither ate nor drank much nourishment and showed little interest in anyone or anything.

As a white candle
In a holy place
So is the beauty
of an aged face.
As the spent radiance
of the winter sun

So is a woman
with her travail done.
Her brood gone from her
and her thoughts as still
As the waters
Under a ruined mill.
—James Campbell

Toward the end of February while we were walking home from school, we met a neighbor on his way to the shop who told us that our grandmother had died earlier that day while we were in school at the ripe old age, in those days, of 86. He told us she was well prepared to go home to God as the priest had visited her that morning and gave her Extreme Unction. It was generally understood that when the priest was spotted going to someone's house, the undertaker would not be too far behind.

Upon hearing the news, we ran home as fast as we could. We were truly upset at hearing of her passing. When we reached our house, some of the neighboring women were already there. We were not allowed to go upstairs to see "Old Mam" because these local ladies were busy washing her body and preparing for her wake and reposing. It was the custom in our part of the country that neighboring women prepared the body, put on the brown habit—some people called it a shroud— and made up the bed where she would repose.

"Old Mam" was laid out in the brown habit of St. Francis in the same bed that she had slept on for many years with me by her side prior to her final days. The fancy bed linens and covers that she had brought from America many years earlier were taken out of the black steamer trunk and put on her deathbed just as she had planned. There, she reposed peacefully and serenely between her lace-trimmed sheets under her camphorated American candlewick bedspread.

That evening relatives, friends, and neighbors came to our house for her wake and to offer their sympathy to my father. I recall her wake being a pleasant occasion, with lots of chit chat, tea, bread, cold meats, and plenty of food as well as Guinness's Stout, Sandeman's Sherry, Lemonade, and Orangeade, snuff for the ladies, and clay pipes for the men to puff on. These customs were said to ward off evil spirits. While snuff and tobacco were expensive items, they were always disseminated and visible at wakes. That was the tradition and nobody wanted to discontinue it, fearing unknown consequences.

The day following her death, her body was removed to the parish church, where it remained overnight. The next day she was buried in the family plot in the local graveyard, next to my grandfather, who had predeceased her more than fifty years earlier. She went to her eternal reward without ever being actually told that her daughter in America had predeceased her. A huge mistake.

My parents were unhappy with the graveyard's policies where "Old Mam" was buried. It was a very old Protestant graveyard with a small section designated for Catholic burials, which surrounded an ancient Church of Ireland (Protestant Church) edifice. For us, when a church was referred to as a church, it was commonly understood that it was not a Catholic Church but a Church of Ireland. In Catholic settings our church was called a chapel. My parents did not want to be buried in a Church of Ireland graveyard, which was always associated with non-Catholics. The former rectors of the church were buried in the immediate vicinity of the church building. Catholics were buried much further back well removed from the line of vision of the wealthier Protestant congregation who attended Sunday services there. The rector, or parson, as he was called, held the key for the gate to the graveyard. He was rarely available during the week to unlock it and allow Catholics access to visit the graves of their deceased family members. My parents felt very uncomfortable and intimidated having to seek out the parson to open the tall wrought iron gate so they could visit "Old Mam's" grave and say a prayer for the repose of her soul. In those days, Catholics and Protestants intermingled with their own congregations only. The rector did not extend a welcome to those who were not members of his congregation.

My parents decided they would not be laid to rest in that graveyard because it was entirely too humiliating and difficult for a person of the Catholic faith to gain access to it when they wanted to visit a grave. A few years later, a new all-Catholic graveyard opened a short distance from our own parish church. My father was among the first to be buried there, followed several years later by my mother.

While "Old Mam" was nearing her own death, and over the course of her wake and funeral, her brother, my granduncle, was also close to death in the other bedroom next to my grandmother's. He had contracted a serious case of pneumonia, which weakened him. He was confined to bed, to recover under my mother's loving care, but he deteriorated rather quickly. He died a short three weeks after my grandmother. My mother and father, with the help of our neighbors, once again proceeded with the same preparations for his wake and funeral as they had just completed for my grandmother.

As a young man, my granduncle was a talented weaver as well as a gifted writer of poetry and rhymes.

99

He enjoyed creating rebuses that were published, together with his poetry and rhymes, in the annual edition of *Old Moore's Almanac*. His weaving projects included making creels, *pardógs, gubawns,* as well as picnic and egg baskets. We used the picnic baskets to carry the tea out to the meadow when my father and brothers were saving the hay.

We used the egg baskets to carry the eggs we were selling to either the local shop or the van man. My granduncle made the baskets by hand from young, pliable sally rods. For creels and *pardógs* he used more mature rods for greater durability and longer life. *Pardógs* were attached to a straddle on the asses' backs and used to transport turf from the bog. Creels were smaller and wider than *pardógs* and had oval shaped bottoms. *Pardógs* were similar only in that they were used for the same purpose as creels but were much deeper, and had square, trap-door bottoms, similar to a large carton. *Gubawns* were used on young calves, as a muzzle, to wean them off their mother and to prevent them from eating weeds and other poisonous plants. They were removed just as soon as the calf matured and developed the ability to differentiate between and among grass, edible plants, and poisonous weeds. Not only was it used as a safety measure, the *gubawn* was another way of training a young calf not to eat between regular feedings.

Following my granduncle's death my entire family was ordered by the local doctor to undergo a series of tests as a precautionary measure to rule out any serious contagious disease as the cause of death, such as tuberculosis, which was rampant in Ireland at that time. This was an arduous undertaking for my father and mother to dress and transport us children, two of them infants, for chest x-rays and appropriate immunizations. Fortunately, and to our parents' great relief, none had contracted any serious disease like the dreaded tuberculosis.

Not only were they relieved at hearing the good news, they were doubly relieved to know that they would not suffer the ugly stigma associated with tuberculosis, known as consumption, in those days. Many unfortunate victims of this dreaded disease were transported by the County Home ambulance and placed in isolation in a sanitarium near the coastline where exposure to salt water and sea breezes was considered a mighty force in the recovery process. Patients suffering from tuberculosis were not allowed visitors because this dreaded disease was so highly contagious and there was always the fear that a visitor might become infected or be a carrier of tuberculosis and contaminate the whole community. The sanitarium that served our area was a long distance from our home and we were indeed blessed that we were neither victims nor carriers of tuberculosis, a truly most dreaded disease in those days.

On the plus side, when "Old Mam" and our granduncle went to their eternal reward, we gained the use of the two additional bedrooms they occupied. During the final stages before they died, they each had their own bedroom, which made it difficult and certainly very crowded for us children and our parents to share the other bedroom, the little room downstairs, and the parlor during that period before God called them to Himself. When the bedrooms where they had died were refurnished, freshly painted, thoroughly disinfected, and aired out, we moved back into them. The bedroom that my granduncle occupied was designated the boys' room and "Old Mam's" room became the girls' bedroom. They remain as such to the present day, filled with memories of laughter and joy, life and death. Oh, only if their walls could talk, what stories they would tell.

The laughter and frivolity we engaged in as young children in those bedrooms gave way to the quiet waiting period of two frail, elderly people who waited for God to call them to His more perfect home. When they passed on to their eternal reward, those bedrooms returned once again to the sounds of life and laughter and the familiar hums that filled their space a couple of generations earlier. A major difference was those sounds now came from vacationing grandchildren and great-grandchildren visiting from near and far to spend some time in the peace and tranquility of their ancestral home down on the farm. Yes, it is indeed a true saying that "life goes on" and, in this particular case, the cycle of life has generously repeated itself in the spirit and rebirth of younger, livelier, and, indeed, more affluent subsequent generations.

Six

The Station

Saint Patrick's Breastplate

Today I put on
the power of Heaven,
the light of the Sun,
the radiance of the Moon,
the splendor of fire,
the fierceness of lightning,
the swiftness of wind,
the depth of the sea,
the firmness of earth
and the hardness of rock.
—Anonymous

The evening before our Station, I was sitting at the kitchen table doing my homework by the glow of the lamplight, when suddenly the tantalizing aroma of baking coming from the scullery broke my concentration and lured me away. I was planning, as soon as my mother's back was turned, to snatch a handful of raisins or a helping of mixed fruit peel, both sitting on the sideboard within my line of vision, but, alas, a few feet beyond my reach. My mother was busy carefully following her recipes and combining the ingredients for the fancy bread that would appear on the breakfast table after the Station Mass the next morning.

I had just turned seven years of age and was too young to be a significant helping hand, yet curious enough not to ignore the hustle and bustle taking place around the house. Like any inquisitive child, as far as my mother was concerned I was more of a hindrance than a help to her. Fearing she would make a mistake, she banished me from the kitchen lest I distract her from following recipes as she carefully measured the ingredients for the special breads she was making for the Station. She rarely used a recipe except on some occasions when the bread and cakes were different and more special than those she made for our everyday consumption. She was vigilant and attentive, making sure she did not make an error at this crucial time with the Station about to take place. The final phase of preparing for neighbors coming to our house for the Station Mass and to partake in the breakfast that followed was close at hand. Since all the major preparations were completed and everything was in place, the baked goods had to be perfect, too.

My mother made all kinds of fancy bread including fruit cakes, whole wheat, raisin with mixed fruit peel, raisin with treacle, ginger and nutmeg, plain, caraway seeded, and of course, the usual Irish soda bread. Exotic varieties and shapes of bread, with combinations of ingredients seldom before seen or rarely heard of, would appear on the breakfast table the morning of the Station. In addition, she made sure a supply of storebought bread was also available. Indeed, she spared no effort.

Instead of snatching a handful of raisins, my mother gave me a stern look—enough said. I got the message; her eyes said it all. It was time to move on and get out of sight as quickly as possible. Nevertheless, I enjoyed and savored the moment as I quietly and inconspicuously loitered about the kitchen, salivating around the doorjamb, eavesdropping on the adult conversation as they exchanged stories and discussed plans for the Station. When the house was fully prepared, both inside and out, baking bread and cakes was the final undertaking. Because refrigeration was not yet an option, baking was done the night before so the bread was fresh and soft.

The weeks and days leading up to the Station were exciting for me and worrisome for my parents; exciting because all the necessary preparations were completed, worrisome lest any detail or precaution be overlooked to cause my parents anxiety or embarrassment. At this point, the eleventh hour, it was not the time for any last minute surprises.

For us children and even for our parents and neighbors, the grandest church related event was the Station, a Catholic ritual unique to rural Ireland and the sadder chapters of its history. This ancient custom was an opportunity for the priest to come to a house in one of the townlands within a parish to celebrate Mass. Our parish was made up of roughly fifteen to twenty townlands. Some were larger in area than others and had from seven to ten families living within their boundaries. A family in each townland within the parish was designated to host the Station in alternating homes every three or four years during either the spring or fall season.

Hosting the Station was a custom that was carried on from the Penal Law era of the 18th century when Catholics were persecuted and priests were forced to say Mass at secret locations in rural Ireland. While similar to Apartheid laws in South Africa, the Penal Laws were aimed solely at persecuting Catholics because of their faith and their purpose was to convert the colonized Irish Catholics to Protestantism. The Apartheid laws were aimed at ethnic groups and races and were not directed at any particular religion.

The sites chosen for the priest to say Mass in those Penal days were shielded by high dense hedges to protect the priest and the congregation from being seen by the enemy and so were known as Hedgerow Masses. As time passed, the Hedgerow became the house and the custom known as the Station began. In our part of the country, the priest would ask the parishioners to let him know which of them would be hosting the Station this time around. Rotation depended upon the number of families within a townland and their willingness to host it. People were painfully slow in volunteering because preparations needed to be undertaken well in advance of the event. Because many households were occupied by either older folk whose children had emigrated, or aging bachelors living alone, whose houses were in poor shape, in the spirit of kindness and consideration, younger neighbors, and those with women in the house, often volunteered even though it was not their turn.

When a neighbor reluctantly volunteered after some coaxing and pleading, that family would immediately begin to decorate and tackle projects in preparation for the big event. Wallpapering the parlor, cleaning windows, washing floors, dusting and removing cobwebs, varnishing and waxing furniture, and working tirelessly to put the house in spic 'n span order for the occasion were some of the jobs undertaken to get ready. These major face-lifting jobs began several months in advance. Anyone strolling by would notice the new lace curtains at the windows, the clean, whitewashed walls, the newly painted gates that led up to the front door, and the spruced-up appearance all around the house. Hedges were neatly trimmed, roses, daffodils, and fuchsia were in full bloom;

potted flowering geraniums were strategically arranged along the perimeter of the house to add a splash of color; shrubs were neatly pruned; and the whole place looked inviting both inside and out for that very special occasion—the Station.

The fine china, serving dishes, and "the good," freshly polished silverware were brought out from their safe-keeping cabinet or velvet-lined chest to be used for the big breakfast to follow the Station Mass. Even the butter was specially made for the occasion. Instead of serving the usual chunk-like block of creamery butter, my mother spent a lot of time molding it into fancy shapes, curly swirls, and decorative little balls, adding a touch of elegance to the breakfast table. The crystal sugar bowl was filled with plenty of lumps, served with small silver tongs, always stored away and brought out only on very rare occasions such as the Station or a wake. Oftentimes, the farmers were defeated in handling the dainty, silver tongs with their big hands and occasionally one of the sugar lumps would soar up and across the table or bounce on the floor beneath it. Of course, the farmers were much more familiar with the standard teaspoon and the usual granulated sugar.

On the big day itself, before the priest and the first group of men were seated around the breakfast table, my mother and those neighboring farmers' wives who were helping her prepare the food would worry and wonder over such problems as whether the priest might like a soft-boiled egg, a fried egg, or a scrambled egg. They would ask one another, "Do you think he'd like a white egg or a brown one?" Then, someone would suggest that "Maybe he'd like a duck egg." And on and on. The worrying and wondering and satisfying the priest, making sure no details were left out, were integral parts of the Station ritual. The meal was not necessarily restricted to the usual breakfast food. Cold meats were often served as well as a variety of desserts.

The host family always faced the major decision of who would be seated next to the priest for the meal. The man of the house was always seated at one side of him, but choosing who would be seated at his other side was a soul-searching decision. There was the fear that if they did not carefully select the most gentlemanly farmer, likely some vulgar, untoward words might slip out and cause embarrassment to the priest and the host family. Another major consideration was that the person seated next to the priest be a good conversationalist, well versed on topics of world interest, local and current affairs, highly respected in the community, and well-known to the priest himself. The man usually deserving this honor would be a father who either had a son who was a priest, or studying for the priesthood, or a daughter who was a nun or about to enter the convent. Next might be the local schoolmaster, a distinguished relative, a visitor from abroad, or someone in a position of status in the area, like the doctor or the vet. If someone in the congregation of local farmers or their wives had a brother or sister in religious life, that would be a big plus, too, and would warrant a place of distinction close to the priest or within earshot of him. The more rough and ready farmers were relegated to seats either much further down the table or were politely asked to wait for the second seating in case the priest should get a whiff of the farmyard from their clothing. God forbid the priest should be exposed to conversations evolving around machinery, livestock, and other related topics and discussions concerning life on the farm. Then, according to custom, my mother and the rest of the women were the last group to be served. They waited until all the men had breakfast before they seated themselves for their breakfast.

Priests were held in such high esteem and reverence that they were considered lord and master over ordinary people. The priesthood in Ireland has always been a special calling. In a poor but devout nation, priests were looked upon not just for spiritual guidance, but for political, social, and moral leadership as well, and they were held in awe by their parishioners. To defy or even to disagree with a priest was to court bad luck in this life and assure damnation in the next.

When our family's turn to host the Station came around and all these concerns were taken care of, my father made sure there was plenty of dry turf on hand to keep a blazing fire going. His favorite was what he called black stone turf. This kind was indeed black and when dried it was hard as coal. Stone turf burned more slowly than white turf and emitted more intense heat. White turf, on the other hand, was generally the first few layers of peat cut and was really nothing more than spongy, wet peat moss that had solidified. It burned quickly and was used mostly as kindling to get the fire going. Once it burned, it produced plenty of soft, fluffy ashes that were used as fertilizer for flowers and young seedlings, but this day was special and so the turf must be also.

The morning of the Station my father arose early, got dressed, and started the fire in the parlor where Mass would be celebrated. He carefully carried red-hot *gríosach* (embers) on the short, stubby shovel from the fireplace in the kitchen to the fireplace in the parlor. He then arranged the turf around the embers until they ignited. Patiently he watched the smoke swirl up the chimney to be sure the flue was clear, making sure it drew the smoke up and out freely. It was not unusual for the flue to be blocked by either a jackdaw's or a crow's nest. Somehow these despicable birds knew the parlor chimney did not regularly puff smoke like the kitchen chimney beside it did. And they were right. The parlor was seldom used except on those rare occasions when we had visitors from abroad (England or America), when there was a wake in the house, or when it was our turn to host the Station. When he was satisfied the fire was burning brightly in the parlor, he then went outdoors to make sure there were no unsightly farmyard droppings in the immediate vicinity. Our house looked inviting indeed when all the preparation and refurbishing were completed. It had been transformed from an ordinary farmhouse into an extraordinary, squeaky-clean showplace. As a final precaution, my father made sure the dog was tied up lest he frighten the priest by his barking and bounding out to greet him.

The evening before our Station, my father and brother picked up the Priest's Box from the former host's house and placed it in our parlor on top of the table, creating the altar the priest would use to say Mass the following morning. The Box contained the altar stone, vestments, robe, and supplies needed for Mass. My mother had already prepared and polished the brass candlesticks for the lighted candles used during the Mass. One lighted candle was placed at each side of the altar as a sign of eternal salvation.

The family hosting the Station was responsible for collecting the Priest's Box. Then, when our Station was over, the next host family came by and brought the Box to their house and so on until everyone slated to have the Station had the Box in their possession prior to the event. The last host family would then bring the box to the presbytery where it was held until the cycle started all over, either the following spring or fall.

The table with the Station Box in place that served as the altar was covered with snow-white starched tablecloths, a crucifix in the center, and two wax candles at either side. The priest usually arrived around 8:00 A.M. My father escorted him to the parlor, where he robed and prepared to hear confessions. There, two chairs were arranged side by side, adjacent to the fireplace. One, the comfortable armchair, was for the priest and the other straight-backed chair was for the penitent. The first people to go to confession were my father and mother followed by those of us children who had made our first Holy Communion. This was a new experience for me, as I had never gone to confession face-to-face before and not only was I somewhat scared of what the priest might say, I was also concerned that he would reprimand my parents about the behavior of their children. All went well, and I later grew to enjoy going around to the local houses when it was their turn to host the Station.

When the priest finished hearing the confessions, he started Mass, which was in Latin at that time. My brother, the altar server who had been learning the Latin responses in preparation for the Station, rendered them appropriately. It was a very solemn occasion as our neighbors, my parents, and all eleven of us children watched the priest sprinkle holy water all around the house while praying for those that had either died or could not be with us for whatever reason. It was both a happy and holy occasion in which neighbors came together in the spirit of prayer and worship, to enjoy each other's company and to bring the blessing of the Station back home with them to their own house and family.

When the Mass was over, it was customary for the priest to collect Station money. The host family was the first contributor and they usually made the most generous donation. This amount was scrutinized closely by those present, and no one in attendance ever gave more than the host family. On the next Sunday following the Station, the list of donors was read from the altar in the parish church so those at Mass could double-check who made a donation and hear how much money they gave.

One Station, in particular, stands out in my mind. It was our neighbor's turn to host it and having gone through the usual preparation and decorating and deciding who would be seated next to the priest, they nervously and expectantly awaited the day and time for the priest to arrive. The local, semi-retired schoolmaster was the person selected to sit next to the priest. Though the obvious choice, this turned into a disaster. Our good-natured neighbor was unaware that the aged schoolmaster had lost the hearing in his right ear, leaving him totally deaf in that ear. As it happened, he was seated to the left of the priest and when the priest engaged him in conversation, the schoolmaster could not hear a word being spoken. Shifting himself from side to side, he occasionally stared into space uttering an occasional, "What was that?" Or "I beg your pardon?" Every once in a while he uttered an occasional, "Huh, I didn't catch that." When someone gave him a kick under the table to get his attention, he turned his chair around, putting its back toward the table, so he could hear what the priest was saying in his "good" ear.

He sat straddling the chair throughout the breakfast, reaching back from time to time to partake in his food and drink his tea. Some people present thought eating with your back to the table was some kind of new style and reserved any comment on it. The reasons for this reserved silence were many, for likely they also suspected that the tufts of bushy hair growing out of his ears had something to do with his hearing problem and silently said a common blessing such as "God bless the mark" or "God be with the days when we were young."

In rural Ireland trepidation often overcame those who saw another person with a malady or handicap of any kind. It was said "Mocking is catching." Any visible abnormality or disfigurement was never mentioned in case it was somehow contagious or for fear some heavier cross might befall those who made fun of the bearer. Since both the schoolmaster and the priest were highly esteemed in the area, the chair switching was accepted as something upper-class people did. No adults made any complaint or spoke a word in case the elderly, semi-retired schoolmaster would take it out on their children or for fear that the long-awaited blessing the priest had brought to the house would become null and void. Nevertheless, this particular incident continued as a hot topic of conversation and at subsequent Stations it was not unusual to see chairs placed so they could easily be switched around to facilitate any unforeseen occurrence or incident.

Immediately following the Mass, the priest blessed a bucket of fresh spring water that was placed alongside the table where he said Mass. A new, white enamel bucket, preferably one with a black trim around the top, was purchased for this very special occasion. Those in attendance would bring a bottle of the holy water home with them to have on hand in their own homes. Farmers used the holy water to bless their family, cattle and farm animals, crops, turkeys, chickens, and indeed anything that moved and some that didn't.

The priest also blessed rosary beads, medals, holy pictures, scapulars, and other religious objects brought by neighbors when the Station was in their townland. Some of the older folks often told us children that we should not let anyone else use our blessed rosary beads because the person using them would win the blessing off the beads and we would not gain any benefit or indulgences from using them ourselves. Occasionally green scapulars appeared among the items to be blessed, but brown ones were by far the more abundant and popular color. It was said, and widely believed, that if you wore the brown scapular when you went swimming you would not drown.

It was a common practice in every household to have a shrine erected in the kitchen displaying pictures of favorite saints, holy medals, and relics of saints. Adjacent to the shrine was a small paraffin oil lamp with a red globe that softly burned before a large picture of the Sacred Heart. This picture bore the family name indicating the family was enrolled in the Society of the Sacred Heart. In addition, a crucifix stood immediately below the Sacred Heart picture. Invariably, there was a picture of Our Lady of Mt. Carmel with the brown scapular dangling from her raised right hand as she cradled the Infant Jesus on her lap with her left arm wrapped securely around His waist. This was a common sight in every home and indeed everyone at the Station was familiar with it. Consequently, wearing the blessed brown scapular was a popular, long-held custom.

The green scapular was lesser known and customarily associated with the French since it was entrusted to Sister Justine Bisqueyburu, a Daughter of Charity of St. Vincent de Paul, in Paris around 1840. The particular power of the green scapular is conversion and to bring the Son of God into the hearts of men. It was a common understanding that you should not purchase a green scapular for your own purposes. Like the Infant of

Prague, which was always given as a gift, the green scapular was also given as a gift. Since everyone at the Station was indeed a devout Catholic, the need for conversion seemed removed and superfluous. As a result, the green scapular was not as popular as the brown.

When the Station Mass and breakfast were finished, the priest visited and brought Holy Communion to the homebound, aged, and infirm people in the townland who were unable to come to Mass that morning. Then, as soon as the priest left our house and the neighbors went on their way, it was time to change clothes and tend to the usual household chores and the farm animals whose normal routines had been so rudely interrupted by the events.

After the Station, our house stood as a shining beacon, both inside and out, a testament to having undergone major overhauling and face-lifting preparations for the recently held Station. An aura of peace and serenity remained within its walls where we peacefully enjoyed the blessing of the Station. Now our house was ready for any unexpected visitors or returning American relatives to drop by. A blessing in its own way, the Station provided an occasion to update and tackle many neglected projects. In that way, it fulfilled material as well as spiritual purposes, perhaps the unspoken intention of the custom.

Indeed, it was not unusual for items to be either misplaced or missing because, in the flurry of preparation, many items were either discarded, misplaced, or relegated to some unknown quarters only to be discovered again when either preparing for the Station the next time around, or many years later.

Having the Station in our home was indeed a very sacred and worthwhile event that fills my heart with many happy memories of blessings and transformations.

Regrettably, the custom ended more than two decades ago due to several factors. Primary among them was increased immigration, which resulted in fewer families available or willing to host it, the abandonment of small farms, and to some degree a shortage of priests.

Nowadays, with advancement and growth in the economy and a decrease in immigration, the automobile has replaced the bicycle and it is the accepted and more popular mode of transportation. Today, people can either drive or be driven to church to attend Mass and receive the sacraments much more frequently rather than waiting around, as they did in time gone by, for a family to host the Station in their townland in order to fulfill their Easter Duty. As economic progress and affluence continue to grow and develop across a very modern, rural Ireland, the local priest uses his own automobile and cell phone to respond to emergencies, attend to sick calls, and bring Holy Communion to the aged and infirm, the homebound, and shut-ins on a regular basis.

Consequently, that memorable custom of hosting the Station in a country farmhouse with family and neighbors as well as all the hectic antecedent preparations, has faded into oblivion and forever gone by way of the historic hedgerow Masses that were secretly celebrated on a rugged, hedgerow Mass rock during that cruel, bygone Penal Law era when Catholics were persecuted for practicing their gift of Catholic faith.

Seven

Teenage Years

Out of the night that covers me,
Black as the pit from pole to pole,
I thank whatever gods may be
For my unconquerable soul.
In the fell clutch of circumstance
I have not winced nor cried aloud.
Under the bludgeonings of chance
My head is bloody, but unbowed.
Beyond this place of wrath and tears
Looms but the horror of the shade,
And yet the menace of the years
Finds and shall find me unafraid.
It matters not how strait the gate,
How charged with punishments the scroll,
I am the master of my fate,
I am the captain of my soul.
—William Ernest Henley

By this time, I had completed the eighth class at our National School and had reached the stage in my young life where I was expected to make a decision about my own goals for the future. My two older sisters were attending secondary school and it was my wish to follow in their footsteps. Our schoolmaster recommended that I take the examination for the county scholarship. This examination was given over a two-day period, in another town about fifteen miles from our home. I was terrified at the thought of being away from home overnight, as I had never been before and the very thought of spending two nights by myself in a town much larger than our local village was a daunting thought.

Early in the morning on the day before the examination, my father and I left home on bicycles and together we cycled up and down hill until we reached the town and the examination site. We went from door-to-door looking for overnight lodgings as close as possible to the exam location. When we finally happened upon possible lodgings, my father did the talking and negotiated the cost of spending two nights with an elderly couple who had a spare room and was willing to accommodate me for the two nights. The lady of the house took me to the room where I would sleep. She invited me to place my personal belongings in an old steamer trunk that served as both a nightstand and a storage chest. On the walls hung several holy pictures including the Sacred Heart, the Blessed Mother, saints, familiar and unfamiliar, a large crucifix, and an empty holy water font hanging from a big rusty nail set into the doorjamb at the entrance. It was a dark and dingy room with a very small window, tattered wallpaper on the walls, and plenty of cobwebs dangling from the ceiling. Several photographs of a young girl were arranged in groups showing various stages of the child's growth and maturity. No matter where I stood in that room, the girl's gaze was fixated on me from every angle. I found the accommodation to be entirely too eerie and I was petrified at the thought of sleeping there alone overnight.

The double bed in the middle of the floor had a dark

wooden headboard carved with shapes of leaves and branches. The mattress, sunken in the center, was covered with a heavy, multi-colored patch quilt. The odor of mold added to the stuffiness of the place and the howling of the mangy, shaggy dog outside the window only added to my apprehension. To compound my nervousness, the lady told me how happy she was to have a young person sleep in that particular room because it had not been used since her fifteen-year-old daughter died in it several years earlier and was laid out to repose on the same bed I would be sleeping on. The still grieving lady took great pride in telling me she had maintained the room in exactly the same way since her daughter's passing, and because I was close to her daughter's age when she died, I reminded her of the youthful, bygone, happier times they shared together. I was quite sure I did, but I was not happy at the thought of being her replacement.

While I was still shaking and trembling with fear, the elderly lady escorted me outside to her back yard, where the water closet, an authentic working toilet with running water, stood. Since I had never seen a real toilet before, I did not know what this new apparatus was or how it worked. I was impressed at the sight and size of the big, white crockery bowl. About three or four inches of water rested at its bottom and along the side hung a length of chain connected to a tank anchored to the ceiling overhead. I instinctively thought what a small spring well this was and wondered how anyone could draw a bucket of water from it. I presumed they used either a mug or a ponger to do so. I recall thinking what a poor water supply they had and how time consuming it must be to fill a bucket or a kettle from such a low water level. At home, I was accustomed to our large spring well where a bucket could be lowered and filled with minimal effort.

As it happened, I needed to go to the bathroom and since I did not know how to use her toilet, I ran toward the back of her garden and crouched behind a dense rhododendron, all the time pathetically confused at the thought of who would ever think of using their spring well as a bathroom facility.

When I went back inside the house, I began to cry. My father asked me what was wrong. I said that I wanted to go home and did not want to stay in that house or bedroom overnight fearing the daughter's ghost was lurking among the cobwebs or in a corner. I knew I would be lonely and frightened. Even though it was daylight, I was overcome with fear and anticipated the girl's haunting look or her banshee's wailing would disturb my sleep during the night. From my earliest memory, I had the company of my parents and my five sisters and brothers at home. The quiet of this dreary place spoke louder than the day-to-day commotion in our house. My father apologized to the lady and thanked her for offering us the overnight accommodation. She understood why I would be lonely since I was accustomed to an active home life with lots of family members around all the time. When she and my father finished their conversation, she offered us tea and scones, expressed regrets that I would not be staying there, and wished us well in our search for a more suitable accommodation.

When we departed, we walked up the street to a convent where the nuns who taught in the adjoining secondary school lived. It was a beautiful Victorian style building with lots of colorful flower beds leading up to the entrance and shrubs in full bloom; beauty, peace, and serenity flourished everywhere. My father rang the doorbell and a young nun dressed in a stiffly starched white head dress and a long navy habit, with the biggest rosary beads I had ever seen dangling from her belt, reaching all the way down to her shoes, greeted us. She invited us inside and asked us to take a seat in the reception room with its comfortable armchairs and sofas, richly carved furniture, and dressers filled with shiny glasses and china, the likes of which I had never seen before. The highly polished furniture, shiny waxed floors, and adjoining peaceful little chapel added to the warmth and welcoming atmosphere.

A short while later, an older nun came in to meet us. Each nun had her own individual assignment. One answered the doorbell, another greeted and entertained visitors, another cooked or cleaned, another did gardening, and on and on. My father explained our predicament and requested overnight lodgings for me in the dormitory where the boarding school students lived. She was only too pleased to oblige and I spent two nights there. For me, this was a most refreshing change from the dreary, dead child's room, whose memory, like those haunting photographs on its walls, was still all too fresh and vivid to me.

During the evening of my second day there, the head groundskeeper and a nun invited me outside to show me their well tended gardens and surrounding property. One of the gardens was a sea of color with flower beds meticulously arranged and roses in full bloom surrounded by neatly trimmed shrubs. A short distance back was a well-cultivated, weed-free, vegetable garden where peas, beans, cabbages, lettuce, beets, carrots, parsnips, and turnips were all at various stages of blossoming and growth. This was the entire year's main vegetable supply source for the nuns and resident students. The gardens and grounds were planted, maintained, and harvested by the sisters who seemed to thoroughly enjoy their labor of love and the fruits of an abundant harvest.

When we finished walking around and viewing the gardens and property, we then moved on to the sisters' graveyard to pray for the souls of the deceased sisters interred there. It was surrounded by a high stone wall with patches of ivy creeping along the top. This high wall blocked the public view of the headstones and graves inside. At the entrance stood a large crucifix with a life-size corpus of Christ crucified. I was taken aback when I noticed several partially dug graves. The groundskeeper explained that each day when a nun arose she went to the graveyard and removed a shovelful of soil from the burial site that would eventually become her own grave and final resting place. Upon seeing so many partially dug graves, this particular graveyard became more somber and sobering than any I had seen before.

Any consideration of my own education was a low priority. The financial drain was too much for my family because they were paying tuition for my two older sisters who were attending secondary school. With a young, large family to feed and clothe, any extra financial income was more urgently needed for survival than the expense of buying another bicycle for me to attend secondary school. As it happened, the manager of the local store, a man held in high esteem in our community, told my father that there was an opening in his shop for an assistant. My father spoke to him about my being available and asked if he would consider giving me the job. He hired me as a junior shop assistant at age fourteen. I was delighted to get the job and the thought of having my own money was both exciting and attractive. My salary was five shillings a week for forty and, many times, fifty hours' work. The store was open from nine in the morning until nine at night, sometimes later, six days a week, and after Mass on Sunday morning, until one or two o'clock in the afternoon. It was a regular meeting and gathering place for the local farmers to exchange greetings, the news of the week, stories, and to purchase groceries.

It was a general store where farmers could obtain a wide variety of products including shovels, spades, rakes, flour, meal, fertilizer, paraffin oil, cement, tea, sugar, bread, butter, bacon, sausages, ingredients for cures, and various items too numerous to mention. As the newest apprentice and lowest ranking employee, I bore the brunt of the heavy, laborious work. Weighing flour, meal, packing shelves, measuring oil, scrubbing the countertop, and washing the floor were part of my daily and weekly assignments. The small salary I earned was a great incentive and gave me a sense of independence and self-worth. I worked in that store for about two and one-half years. At that point, and I was satisfied that I had gained sufficient experience and competency as a shop assistant. I resigned my job to join my older sister, who was working in Dublin under much better conditions and earning a higher salary for fewer hours' work. She found a job for me as an assistant in a large, modern general store. Together we had a very memorable time in Dublin going to the zoo, Phoenix Park, St. Stephen's Green, shopping, dancing, and high stepping at ceilies on Sunday afternoons. In Dublin, ceilies were dances; unlike Leitrim, where they were known as informal social visits. On our day off, we often went to the pictures or walked around the city enjoying the buildings and the sights from atop the double-decker buses and Nelson's Pillar (now long since gone). During the summer we spent our free time walking on the bulwark at Donnybrook, taking in the sights of the coastline and the seashore. Beachgoers, huddled together in heavy clothing, sat on the beach braving the wind gusts that blew off the Irish Sea even in mid-summer. Weather patterns then were typically partially sunny days and occasional showers, which were not conducive to sunbathing. Even though Ireland continues to get its share of rain throughout the year, summertime in later years is warm and sunny. This weather pattern reversal is now a major attraction for the tourist and visitor industry.

My sister lived upstairs from her place of employment. She enjoyed well appointed private accommodations with a modern adjoining bathroom and a constant supply of hot and cold running water. I found living accommodation, or digs, as it was called, with an older widow woman who lived immediately across the street from where my sister worked and lived. This old lady was lonely and alone. She spent a lot of time musing about her only daughter who had immigrated to South Africa several years earlier. I feared she would perceive me as her replacement. This was not the case at all; in fact, she was always cheerful and gracious. She was very kind and took care of me like a mother. I was delighted that I did not have to rekindle those haunting memories and photographs of a dead child that were etched in my memory from earlier years. She cheerfully prepared and served my meals for the modest sum of thirty shillings a week.

Her favorite dish was the "Dublin Coddle," a dish dating back to the 18th century and unique to native-born Dubliners. I had never heard of or sampled a "coddle" and I awaited her favorite dish with much trepidation. Because she lived alone prior to my arrival, she longed for the day when she could make and share a "coddle." The word "coddle" means to cook slowly or par-boil. The ingredients for a "coddle" recipe include ham, sausages, onions, and potatoes combined with one and one-half pints of water, salt, pepper, and chopped parsley. To the water are added eight thick slices of ham, cut into chunks, eight pork sausages, cut into thick slices, two large onions, peeled and sliced, one and one-half pounds of potatoes, peeled and sliced, salt and pepper and two heaping tablespoons of fresh, chopped parsley.

The first step is to bring the water to a boil in a large saucepan, add the ham and sausages, and cook for five to ten minutes. Drain well, reserving the cooking liquid. Set oven at 300 degrees Fahrenheit. Place the ham and sausages in an ovenproof dish, add the potatoes, seasoning, and chopped parsley, and pour in just enough cooking liquid to cover. Cover with greaseproof paper, put the lid on, and cook for one to one and one-half hours or until the liquid is greatly reduced and the vegetables are cooked. Serve with garnished parsley and Irish soda bread.

This was a common and economical dish in Dublin, particularly for a large family. She insisted upon giving me her deceased mother's recipe, but regrettably, and maybe to my good fortune, I have never used it—so much for a "Dublin Coddle." "I'll have the Boxty!"

At that time, I was earning five pounds a week and I had money left over for shopping, entertainment, and discretionary spending—a newly found luxury indeed. My sister too had extra money to use at her own discretion as well. On our day off, we frequently traveled to the center of the city. We browsed in shop windows; treated ourselves to ice cream cones or sundaes at Cafola's Cafe on O'Connell Street, the main street in the heart of the city; and tea and scones at Bewley's on Grafton Street, the shopping mecca of the city. When the weather was warm and pleasant, we strolled leisurely around St. Stephen's

Green watching artists turn a blank canvas into a sea of color, listening to the fortune tellers who read tea leaves, watching scam artists using sleight of hand as they demonstrated their card games, observing vendors, and street singers plying their trades and peddling their wares. Frequently heard in the background were the familiar Irish tunes "Cockles and Mussels" and "Dublin in the Rare Old Time" being played and sung by a group of local street urchins on the bandstand near the entrance to the park.

On one of our memorable shopping expeditions, having saved enough money for a major purchase, we each bought ourselves new coats. Before we left the shop, we asked the saleslady if she would hold on to our old coats so we would be spared the burden of carrying large packages. We assured her that we would pick them up later on. She was only too willing to accommodate our request. We then quickly removed our old coats and put on the new ones. With chins cocked, we gave ourselves a final look over in the mirror to appreciate the effect and take a good look at ourselves before we went for our stroll. Upon leaving the shop, we walked down O'Connell Street, proud as peacocks, feeling very fashionable in our new attire. I recall how pleased and happy we both were wearing our new coats, all the time thinking how great we looked and how self-assured we were in wearing them.

We strolled around the city for more than an hour often stopping at shop windows to catch a glimpse of ourselves, from different angles, in the reflection of the glass. When we walked over O'Connell Bridge, a sidewalk photographer snapped our photograph. That convinced us all the more how special we looked. We had several copies of the photograph made which we passed around to the other members of our family. For us, they served as a reminder of the day we bought our very first new coats. We were truly elated with our very own purchases. At last, we were rid of the hand-me-down clothing of our earlier childhood years while growing up on the farm in County Leitrim.

My coat was a hundred percent Donegal tweed with a velvet collar that served as protection from the stiff breezes as they whipped around the street corners, well remembered by Dubliners. That coat would serve as protection from the cold and wind. Of course, in those days, there was no such thing as synthetic fabric like polyester. Ladies clothing was made from either wool or cotton and invariably men's suits and top coats were made from long-lasting navy blue serge and heavy duty tweed. I was very careful each time I wore my coat to avoid stains or soiling. I planned to wear it when I immigrated to America in the not too distant future. My sister's coat, a deep shade of blue, was also warm and wooly. She too was cautious while wearing it, always careful to prevent signs of wear and tear, because buying a new coat was a major expense and she too expected to use it for several additional years.

As a rule, we went home for a summer holiday and the Christmas break. The scenic train trip through the heart of Ireland on our way to Leitrim took about two and one-half to three hours. While chugging along, we whiled away the time discussing life in the big city and our own plans for the future. Indeed, we looked forward to spending time at home enjoying our mother's cooking, the love our family shared, chatting with neighbors, and catching up with former school mates, as well as local events like births, deaths, and marriages, that took place when we were away. One Christmas I went home alone. My sister had fallen ill and was unable to accompany me. She spent a couple of weeks in bed with stubborn bronchial congestion that would not clear up. Immediately before Christmas, she was hospitalized and diagnosed with a severe case of pleurisy. It took several additional weeks' hospitalization for her to fully recover. Everyone at home, and particularly my mother and father, were terribly upset and disappointed that she was not with the family for Christmas.

When I returned to Dublin after the break I immediately went to the Richmond Hospital to see how she was progressing. She was teary-eyed and in a lot of pain, telling me that the doctor had plunged a long needle into her chest earlier that morning to drain fluid off her lung. Using her hands to demonstrate the size of the syringe, she compared it to the size of a bicycle pump. She looked so alone and pathetic lying there on a black wrought-iron hospital bed in a crowded ward that reeked from the smell of disinfectant and ether emanating from a nearby operating room.

There were roughly ten other patients, young and old, with a variety of ailments in the ward with her. Some beds had screens drawn around them. My sister told me that meant those patients were either close to death or were already dead and screens were a "Do Not Disturb" signal. While she was hospitalized, she acquired a craving for cooked ham and Cadbury Chocolate. The hospital food was not very palatable and she yearned for a salty or sweet treat. When I visited her, I invariably smuggled in a slice or two of ham and an occasional Kit-Kat or Cadbury Milk Chocolate bar for her enjoyment. Her face would light up with delight when I presented her with the longed for goodies.

Several weeks later, when she acquired more strength, she was discharged from the hospital and went home to convalesce, gain weight, and recover completely under the love and care of my mother and father, which she did, thanks be to God.

I worked in Dublin for a little over two years. At that time my oldest sister had finished secondary school and immigrated to America. She was quite lonely and missed home very much. She lived with our aunt in Brooklyn. One day, my father asked me if I would go over to America to keep her company. When she wrote letters home, she indicated how lonely she was and how much she missed her siblings and the warmth and support of a large family in a home that was always filled with laughter, love, and activity. My sister, who had had the pleurisy, would surely not pass the required stiff medical examination because it had left a scar on her lung and, as a result, she would be immediately rejected. Because of that, I was designated the next logical choice.

Since I was probably the most adventurous girl in our family, I was delighted to hear about the possibility of going to America. It sounded so exciting; I couldn't wait to start the process to go there as soon as possible. That process included getting a small pox vaccination, obtaining a passport, getting finger-printed and having a full medical examination by a team of doctors at the American Consulate in Dublin. Having fulfilled all these preliminaries, I was finally given an all-clear and I immigrated to America in June 1957.

While I was nevertheless excited about going to the U.S., at the same time I was heartbroken and frightened at the thought of leaving my parents and siblings. On the morning of my leaving home, I arose early to the sobbing and crying of my little brothers and sisters pleading with me not to go so far away. My mother prepared me a hearty breakfast. My parents, brothers, and sisters joined me for the meal. I took one bite of the food, but, unfortunately, I could not swallow it because I had such an out of control case of butterflies in my stomach and a constriction in my throat that I gave up trying to get the food down. As I fought back tears, knowing my mother had prepared a special meal, I told her I wasn't very hungry and assured her I would eat later in the day. She instinctively knew my nerves were frazzled and fortunately for me she did not force me to eat.

When the hired car that would take me to the airport arrived at our door, my heart raced and started to beat faster. I knew the moment I most dreaded had arrived and it was now time to say goodbye to my brothers, sisters, mother, and father. Tears flowed, hugs abounded, and at last I was on my way. I wanted to make as fast an exit as possible because listening to and watching my mother, father, brothers, and sisters sobbing and crying was a heartbreak worse than a wake. When the car pulled away from our back door, I looked through the rear window of the car and saw my broken-hearted father standing outside our house waving his white handkerchief and tears streaming down his face. My mother was too distraught to come into view. A few minutes after the car that would take me to the airport sped away and our home faded from view, I regained composure and braced myself amid mixed emotions for my long journey across the Atlantic Ocean to New York. With a heavy heart beating within my chest I boarded the plane for the short flight from Dublin to Shannon Airport, where I would embark on my trans-Atlantic flight to New York. As I climbed the stairs, I remembered the words of a mournful Irish song:

Oft, in the stilly night
Ere slumber's chain has bound me.
Fond memory brings the light,
Of other days around me;
The smiles, the tears of boyhood years,
The words of love then spoken;
The eyes that shone, now dimm'd and gone,
The cheerful hearts now broken! . . .
—Thomas Moore

I arrived at Kennedy Airport, then called Idlewild, at 3:00 o'clock in the morning following a sixteen-hour trans-Atlantic flight on KLM Royal Dutch Airlines from Shannon to New York. My bleary-eyed sister and her equally tired boyfriend met me at the airport. On our way out of the airport terminal, as I reached for the knob on the exit door, to my utter amazement the door automatically opened before me. I was stunned, and, for a moment, I was convinced, never having had any experience with an automatic door before, that I had somehow magically walked through it unscathed. What a rude awakening indeed! That was the very first experience and memory I have of landing in America.

Fortunately my sister's boyfriend owned a car and he drove us from the airport to our aunt's apartment on 8th Avenue in the Park Slope section of Brooklyn. There, I just collapsed on the bed feeling exhausted from the eternally long flight. Next morning, I woke up to a bright sunny day; a most pleasant and refreshing change from the cloudy, damp Irish weather. My sister and I took a short walk around the neighborhood. I was surprised to see trees, grass, and beautiful flowers growing. From my earliest memory, I had never seen pictures of any kind of greenery in New York. When my aunts sent photographs home, the background scenery invariably included images of tall concrete or glass buildings, row houses, cement sidewalks with concrete stoops leading up to the front door of the brownstone house where they lived, and tall, wrought iron fences separating concrete backyards from their adjoining neighbors. There was never a hint of greenery visible. Needless to say, I was surprised to see tall trees, flowers, roses, and many varieties of shrubbery in full bloom as well as green grass, lush and plentiful, in what I had visualized as a totally barren, concrete city.

I spent my first week in New York adjusting to jet lag and getting acquainted with my new neighborhood as well as trying to establish a sense of location. What was north and south in Ireland were the direct opposite in Brooklyn. This was when my father's advice served me very well. He was very diligent about telling us when we were quite young that if we ever got lost or could not find our way, we should look toward the sun's location, assuring us that the sun always arose in the east and set in the west. From the position of the sun we could establish both our direction and location.

As soon as I was somewhat acclimated to my new surroundings, my sister and I went shopping at A & S's department store in downtown Brooklyn. We rode the Seventh Avenue subway from Grand Army Plaza to Hoyt Street. As I looked around at the other passengers on the train, I was amazed to see how many wore glasses. For the most part, the only people in Ireland who wore glasses were old-age pensioners and, even then, they rarely wore them in public. I was amazed, too, at the number of children wearing bands of wire wrapped around their teeth. This was a new observation for me as children back home did not have metal bands around their teeth. With the advancement of medical and dental care in Ireland nowadays, it is not unusual now to see youngsters wearing braces to correct overbites and straighten teeth before they reach adulthood. In the U.S. dental care and hygiene were much higher priorities. During my childhood days, growing up in Ireland, when anyone had a toothache or a problem with teeth, the standard solution was for the dentist to pull the tooth out. Correcting overbites, filling cavities, and other forms of cosmetic dentistry were unheard of at that time; extraction was the usual treatment.

Riding the subway for the first time was a very different experience compared to riding on the train back home in Ireland. The very thought of the subway traveling at high speed underground was distantly removed from the wide open space of the Irish countryside where trains smoothly chugged their way through the green fields passing small villages and towns along the way. The passengers on the subway were a combination of people varying in race and skin color, as well as weight and height. None of them talked to any of their fellow passengers. This, too, was very different from riding the train back home. When taking the train from Dublin to Leitrim, passengers usually engaged one another in conversation which made the trip seem shorter and the time pass more quickly. On the subway in New York everyone seemed to be engaged in his or her own surroundings, either reading advertisements above the seats, newspapers, books, or just staring blankly into empty space. There was no interaction whatsoever except for an occasional "excuse me" when the train jolted causing a rider to bump into another fellow passenger. There were no underground trains in Ireland and the feeling of being underground on a noisy subway, with artificial lighting, traveling at a high rate of speed, among a group of strangers, was totally new and indeed quite frightening for me.

My second week in the U.S. was quite exciting as I looked forward to meeting my other aunt who lived on Long Island. My sister and I rode the Long Island Railroad to Bay Shore, where I would meet her and her family for the first time. This train was much more comfortable and faster than the trains in Ireland. It was cleaner, quieter and more inviting than the underground subway in New York City. My aunt was a pretty lady, with curly auburn hair and deep blue eyes. She had never gone back to Ireland since the day she left more than thirty years earlier. She was very Americanized with no hint of an Irish accent. Her husband was born and raised in Brooklyn. Together they had one daughter who was a few years younger than me. She was in high school and did not have very much in common with her new Irish cousins. We grew up in an entirely different culture and lifestyle. This was the aunt my grandmother, her mother, had so affectionately talked to me about during my early childhood. The one with the lovely curly hair and lots of intelligence—qualities "Old Mam" had attributed to me.

My aunt lived in a big, old-fashioned, center hall, colonial house situated by a lake in an upscale area on the south shore of Long Island. Immediately behind the house was a well maintained and manicured rolling lawn that extended from the back of the house down to the water's edge. It was a beautiful, bucolic setting with ducks on the lake, flowering shrubs, mature tall trees, well-tended, colorful flower beds, neatly trimmed hedges, and gardens cultivated in perfect symmetries. The rows of pansies and marigolds looked artificial in their perfectly laid out arrangements. During the first few days at my aunt's home, I enjoyed this mansion of a house, larger than any I had seen in Ireland, with its tall floor to ceiling

134

windows and separate rooms for each member of her family as well as guest quarters with private bathrooms for visitors.

I spent a lot of my daytime hours outdoors basking in the warm sunshine, by the water's edge, feeling like I was on vacation at a luxurious holiday resort. Having settled in and caught up on jet lag, my aunt took me to the hair salon for my first American haircut and initiation into using scented shampoo and hair conditioner.

When we returned home she prepared lunch. It consisted of a wedge of cantaloupe, which I had neither seen nor tasted before, as well as some perfectly shaped brownish colored sausages. When I saw the sausages, I began to salivate as I had not had a sausage since I left Ireland and I was eager to sample them. They looked so appealing and appetizing, I couldn't wait until they were cooked so I could eat 'em up. She asked me how many of these good looking sausages I would like, and since I was so excited at the very look of them, I said that I would like two. From childhood, I had heard that everything in America was bigger and better than what we were used to back home in Ireland, and indeed I was ready for a wonderful treat. She prepared the two sausages and placed them on a plate in front of me. Filled with anticipation, when I started to eat them, I almost gagged when I tasted them. They did not taste anything like the sausages I was accustomed to. Amid gagging, heaving, and chewing, I suffered through until I finally consumed the last piece. The tall glass of iced tea she had offered me was much appreciated and helped me get rid of the very overpowering taste. It was instilled in us from an early age that we should finish whatever it was we started— that also applied to food, so, of course, I was trapped. With a rude awakening and to my dismay, I learned they were not sausages at all, but frankfurters. That was my first and last experience with them. From that day to this day, I have not eaten a frankfurter—the taste still lingers on.

Now that the lunch disaster was over, I wondered what would be on the menu for dinner. As mid-afternoon approached, my aunt started to plan the menu and set the table for dinner. She cooked a large piece of roast beef, which smelled wonderful, as it roasted in the oven. When we were seated for dinner, she asked me to fetch the gravy boat. I was only too happy to offer whatever assistance I could and immediately went out to find the gravy boat. When I did not return after several minutes she went to the kitchen and got the gravy boat herself. She was shocked to notice that I was not there; instead, I was outside, down by the lake shore looking diligently for a boat and wondering how I could manage to bring it into the house and how in God's name was she planning to put it on the table, which was already set for dinner. In Ireland, the gravy container was called a gravy bowl, so calling it a boat was totally new to me.

The following day she took me shopping for suitable business attire. Once inside the store, I was amazed at its very size. There were racks upon racks of dresses long and short, formal and informal, suits, jackets, coats, blouses, skirts, all available in a wide variety of sizes and colors, solids and prints, the likes of which I had never seen before. This was truly a feast for my eyes. I did not know what to look at first. There was just so much to see and select from. It was an overwhelming switch from the one-of-a-kind clothing shops that were available back home. She bought me appropriate business clothing, shoes, a pocketbook, which was not a book at all, but, what in Ireland was called a handbag, as well as accessories suitable for a job interview and ultimately for obtaining a job in the business world.

Now that I had a new wardrobe and all the attending accessories necessary for work in the world of banking and finance, I was appropriately attired and up to the challenge as well as mentally ready to find a job and take my place as a productive, self-sufficient member of this new society I had recently adopted. The time had come to cast aside the heavyweight woolies of Ireland saturated with the sweet smell of purple heather and warm turf fires and make my debut, dressed like the natives, in my new brightly colored, lightweight fashions, feeling more like I belonged, at least outwardly and for that moment, in the big city of New York. Now that those requirements and details were taken care of, I was very excited and confidently ready to find a suitable job and enter the world of work. The next move was up to me.

Eight

Coming to America

From the Song of the Open Road

Afoot and light-hearted, I take to the open road,
Healthy, free, the world before me,
The long brown path before me,
leading wherever I choose.
—Walt Whitman

As a youngster, I had often heard that the streets of New York were paved with gold, and having good eyesight myself, I did not stumble upon or spot any of those elusive nuggets during my first couple of weeks in the U.S.

My sister, who was living in Brooklyn, was employed at a large bank on Wall Street. Since she was able to find her own way when she came to the U.S., I was quite confident that I, too, would be equally capable of following in her footsteps. Even though I had limited skills and was raised within limited means, my head was filled with unlimited dreams and lofty aspirations. With confidence and resolve, I was determined to obtain a job in either a large bank or financial institution.

On Monday of my third week in the United States, my sister and I took the subway from Brooklyn to Wall Street in downtown Manhattan to look for employment. She accompanied me to show me the way so I would be capable of making the commute on my own. It was a relatively short trip from Brooklyn to the financial district and Wall Street at the tip of Manhattan.

Our first stop was at the Chemical Corn Exchange Bank on Broad Street. We rode the elevator to the Personnel Office on the 11th floor, where I began the process of carefully filling out a series of employment application forms. With the assistance of my sister, I managed to complete them quickly and accurately. Following a lengthy interview with one of the personnel officers, I was hired as a clerk. Since I was not familiar with U.S. currency, it was highly unlikely I would be given a position in any area that involved financial matters. I accepted the job and started to work the following week. It was a somewhat frightening experience for me starting a new job, in a large bank, where I knew nobody. The department where I was assigned had a staff of about 200 to 250 employees, all holding various positions. More than two-thirds were men and the balance was made up of older single women (all old maids) and young girls, many recent high school graduates. Fortunately for me, there was another girl from Ireland working in the department. We were in similar situations because she, too, was a recent arrival to the U.S. and had not yet established friendships with many people. Like magnets attracting, we teamed up, ate lunch together, and enjoyed each other's company. It was wonderful to share a touch of home with someone who understood my cultural background and shared my interests.

On payday, we often went on shopping trips together. In the vicinity, there were many clothing, shoe, and jewelry stores, as well as variety and specialty shops. One particular payday, I did some shopping on my lunch hour. When I returned to the office with my bulging bag I was amazed at how many of the girls asked to see what I had in it. When I told them it contained messages, they looked at me in a most peculiar way. Messages in the U.S. meant brief, written notes usually related to telephone calls, or short office memos requesting either action or a reply, whereas messages in Ireland was a word used to describe smaller, lightweight items purchased in either a clothing, grocery store, or specialty shop. Of course, I did not understand the unusual stares I got when I said I had messages in my shopping bag. A short while later, one of the girls finally asked me, through much giggling: "Who sent you the messages?" It was only then I realized the conflict in the meaning of the word.

Between the confusion over the messages and the audacity of someone asking me what was in the bag, I became flustered and wanted to go back home to Ireland where language interpretation wasn't a barrier and everyone understood one another. There, no one would ever ask you direct questions or inquire about what you had purchased. That was considered being inquisitive and obnoxious. In the U.S. it was an occasion to get compliments and comments on purchases and not intended, as I had understood, to imply probing or delving into personal business. As time passed, I grew accustomed to talking more openly with the girls about what I had bought and they usually shared their opinion on my purchases as I did on theirs. Today, I, too, would consider it hilarious if someone told me they had messages in a big, brown shopping bag with the store's logo emblazoned on the outside, similar to the one I was using back then. The laughter we shared then continues to echo in my ears across the years.

I caught on rather quickly to the U.S currency system

and having mastered the clerical responsibilities of my job, I enrolled in typing and shorthand classes, which were offered by the bank free of charge following regular working hours. It took me roughly three or four months to master typing fast enough to pass the qualifying test, which fortunately I did the first time around. Having done that, I qualified to be placed as a typist within the department where I worked. I always kept my ears open, listening for any upcoming job promotions or vacancies I would be interested in applying for. Having a good head for numbers and the ability to calculate quickly and accurately, I was offered a promotion to work in the bank's portfolio department. It was there that the department manager assigned me the task of calculating the sales of stocks and bonds for the traders. Because of my earlier training calculating and adding up figures and prices quickly when I was a shop assistant back home, I enjoyed this new challenge and did it speedily and accurately. It was very exciting watching the fluctuations of the ticker tape while quickly calculating the purchases and sales, as well as the profit and loss of the stocks and bonds as it ticked by.

As soon as I became proficient at typing and the aspects of calculating stocks and bonds trades, I enrolled in evening classes and worked toward obtaining a NYS high school diploma. My days were filled with work, my evenings with learning and studying, and my weekends were a time for fun, dancing, and enjoyment. When I completed the high school preparatory course, I took the comprehensive examination for the high school diploma. This examination was given over the course of two days at Erasmus Hall High School in Brooklyn. For me, it was quite a demanding examination as the format was very different from what I had been accustomed to in Ireland.

The anxiety of waiting for the results from the New York State Board of Education was overwhelming. Several weeks following the examination, a large brown envelope addressed to me finally came in the mail. I nervously opened it and to my surprise and delight there was the fancy engraved New York State Board of Education Regents High School Diploma. I was truly elated and delighted that my hard work and sacrifice had paid off. There was another type of high school diploma available called the GED. To earn this particular diploma, preparation and study were neither as demanding nor time-consuming as the prerequisites for the more widely recognized New York State Regents Diploma—the one I wanted, and the one I got.

While attending evening school in preparation for my high school diploma examination, I met and made friends with other Irish girls who came from different parts of Ireland. We chatted about our homeland, jobs, studies, goals, and our social life. Conversation usually began with finding out what county the other person came from. When I happened to meet someone from my own county, I usually followed up with more questions to find out the exact vicinity like parish, village, and finally townland.

Once in a while I would meet and know someone from home if they came from a radius of less than twenty miles from our house. Of course, in the late 1950s, twenty miles was a long distance uphill and down dale in rural Ireland. In those days, anyone coming from a distance beyond that to which you could cycle were strangers. For the most part, transportation was by bicycle and you would only know those families living within cycling range.

One of the girls I became friendly with was a registered nurse in Ireland. She could not get a nursing job in the U.S. even though she had completed both secondary and nursing school. A nurse without a high school diploma from an accredited high school in the U.S. did not qualify for a nursing position. Her only alternative to work at her profession was to accept a position in the admitting office at Beth Israel, a local Jewish hospital. It was her long range plan to join the nursing staff at that hospital just as soon as she obtained her U.S. high school diploma.

One day, in the course of her normal admitting routine, an elderly gentleman with a full-face beard and a small, round, beanie-style cap sitting on the crown of his head came into her office to be admitted. She was responsible for completing the voluminous paperwork for incoming patients. In the process of filling out the forms, she asked the old man what his Christian name was. Of course, in Ireland, everyone was known by either their Christian name or their surname. Well, the old man immediately became irate, screaming, yelling, and swinging his walking stick in the air saying, "I'm a sick man. Did you hear what she asked me? Did you hear that . . . ? What! What . . . " And on and on. "Can you imagine how I feel? I'm a generous benefactor here and she asks me for my Christian name." Not knowing he was an Orthodox Jew, never having seen a Jewish person before, she didn't know she should not ask for the Christian name when completing paperwork that required a first name. She was fearful beyond words and dreaded being fired if the old man reported her to the hospital administration when she asked him what his Christian name was.

Another girlfriend, also a nurse, applied for a job at a different hospital and, in the course of the hiring process, the interviewer asked her if she suffered from any allergies—particularly to bee stings. She looked at him quizzi-

143

cally and with great sincerity said, "God, I haven't had them in years." The interviewer looking perplexed as his mind raced trying to understand what she was talking about, wondered why she was acting in such a confused manner. He was sure just about everyone had heard of bee stings. When she heard the words bee stings she thought of the "beastings" she was most familiar with, which is the first milk a cow or heifer produces following the birth of a calf. This first milk is rich in vitamins, proteins, and other body building components. In rural Ireland, it was a common practice to feed "beastings" to young children as a tonic. Naturally, when asked if she was allergic to bee stings she instinctively thought of the "beastings" she remembered from her childhood. After a brief discussion and some explaining, they were both enlightened. Together they resolved the bee stings, "beastings" issue and while they shared a hearty laugh, she never forgot the incident. The outcome of her interview was rewarding. She was hired as a nurse at that hospital.

The two most frequently used disinfectants in Ireland were Jeyes Fluid and TCP. Jeyes Fluid was a strong, commercial disinfectant while TCP was a milder product used for wounds that had festered, minor scratches, skin abrasions, and the like. When another girl from home developed a stubborn infection under her fingernail, she went to the local drug store to purchase a bottle of TCP. When added to hot water, and the infected area is soaked in it, TCP will impede and drain the infection and a fast recovery is assured. The druggist, thinking she said STP, a gasoline additive at that time, directed her to a gas station. The druggist thought she was a little wacky trying to purchase STP at a drug store and the gas station attendant thought she was totally nuts trying to purchase TCP at a gas station.

On weekends, my girlfriends and I usually went dancing at the City Center Ballroom, the Jaeger House, or the Tuxedo Ballroom, all of them located in mid-Manhattan. Dressed in our high heels and fancy dresses, we rode the subway from Brooklyn to the dance halls. At City Center, we swayed and swooned to the strains of the Brendan Ward Orchestra with its famous accordion player, Paddy Noonan. As soon as Paddy tickled the keys for an "Old Time Waltz," "The Siege of Ennis," "The Stack of Barley," or the "Rakes of Mallow," we were out on the dance floor high stepping and hopping around to the tempo. When it came time for a lady's choice, we usually took off for the ladies' room rather than ask someone to dance because this was not done in Ireland. Gentlemen invited the ladies onto the dance floor, not the other way around. The practice of ladies asking gentlemen was foreign to our custom and we were not comfortable with this new practice. We had many good times at the Irish dance halls where we met other Irish boys and girls, exchanged stories, and danced the night away. We enjoyed the feeling of camaraderie and the solidarity we shared in New York—a long way from our home. Of course, in Ireland, one did not need to think about or look for solidarity, everyone there was Irish and understood the native social customs and each other's ways. Nowadays, these Irish dance halls are but a memory. Sadly, they are replaced with bar hopping, singing pubs, and cohabitation.

Another Irish-born girl from the high school preparation course met her future husband at City Center Ballroom. He, too, was born and raised in Ireland. Together they made their home in South Brooklyn where they raised their family. Their firstborn child, a darling little boy, was rather puny and small for his age. My girlfriend recalled her mother having fed her a teaspoonful of cod liver oil every morning before she went to school. Remembering this was good for her, she got the bright idea to buy cod liver oil, follow her mother's tradition, and give it to her rather delicate son. So, off she went to the drug store to buy it. The druggist, upon hearing her request, said "This will do the trick." With a raised eyebrow, she looked at him quizzically wondering to herself "How does he know what I want it for?" He told her cod liver oil was great for giving a sheen to a dog's coat and asked if she was raising thoroughbreds. He went on to tell her if more dog breeders had the good sense to use it they would save themselves a bundle of money on special pet shampoos and unnecessary veterinary bills. She was puzzled and embarrassed at hearing this because she did not know cod liver oil was used for any purpose other than as a tonic for delicate, pre-school children.

Another event that comes to mind concerns an entire family from my hometown that immigrated to the U.S. a short time before I did. The family consisted of the father, mother and four children—two boys and two girls. The mother had a difficult time adjusting to the pace of life in New York City. She longed for the day when the family would return once again to the peace and tranquility of their Irish country home surrounded by the open space and fresh green fields, where she watched the rabbits scurry about as the rain fell softly all around. The unique aura and unity of her parish and homeland were very dear to her heart. Her new lifestyle, with the concrete streets and glass skyscrapers of New York City, was in sharp contrast to the scenes of her youth. She had a difficult time adapting to city life and often felt intimidated and overwhelmed as she tried to get accustomed to such a large, crowded city.

Fortunately, she already had a married sister living in New York City who coached her in its way of life. One day, for a change of pace, she treated her newly arrived sister to a movie. Of course, this was the first time her immigrant sister had ever been to a movie theater. The inside of the cinema was quite dark with small, dim lights illuminating the aisles and outlining the edge of the velvet curtain that was drawn shut in front of the screen. As they approached the row where they had decided to sit, the newly arrived sister stopped, genuflected, and reverently made the Sign of the Cross before she quietly took her seat, all the time thinking she was in a church. The only other building of that proportion she had ever been inside of in Ireland was indeed her local parish church.

She settled herself comfortably into her seat and patiently awaited the action of the World War II movie about to unfold before her eyes. Just as she was getting into the story and focusing on the plot, two fighter war planes vrrr-oomed loudly across the big screen. She jumped to her feet screaming loudly as she bolted toward the door. She yelled, "Oh, God, have mercy on us all! That's it. They're going to get us." She was convinced the two planes were coming through the wall in her direction and she ran for her life to get out of their way. Then, turning to her very embarrassed sister, she asked "What are you trying to do to me? Why in God's name did you take me to this place? Do you want to get us both killed or what?" Not only did she create a scene, she rudely interrupted the concentration of the other movie patrons who were stunned by her action and reaction. After much persuasion and hand-holding, she regained her composure and returned to her seat, where she settled down and watched the movie to the end.

As they were leaving the theater, the married sister asked her if she needed to use the restroom. Astounded and surprised at the suggestion, she quickly retorted, saying, "I'm not tired. Weren't we just sitting down in there for a couple of hours? What makes you think I'd be tired? We haven't walked more than a hundred yards from those seats back there Why, are you tired? Indeed, I often walked several miles at home and I didn't feel the least bit tired, and if I did, I'd just look around me and sit down in a comfortable spot and rest for a while. Don't you remember how we walked miles as children to and from school every day, to Mass on Sunday and to town to get the groceries? It would take more than those few steps to make me tired. I am wearing a good pair of walking shoes and I could continue for many more hours before I'd need to rest. If you don't mind me asking, did something happen to you since you came to America that tires you out so quickly when you have been sitting in those comfortable, red velvet seats for a couple of hours?"

When her sister explained what a restroom was, she said "Well, well that's the most absurd name I have ever heard for a toilet." Giggling to herself, she spurted out, "I don't understand why people would want to rest in a place like that." Continuing on with her spiel, she asked "if they don't know why they need to use the toilet, why would they or anyone else need to rest before attending to their business?" In desperation she recommended, "that they should go home and lie down for a couple of hours instead of looking to rest in such a public place. Have they no shame in themselves at all?" Of course, to her, back home responding to nature's call was strictly a private and unmentionable matter and, in her opinion, using a restroom did not seem to be the place to attend to those needs. She was familiar with the more commonly used names like lavatory, outhouse, toilet or bathroom—restroom had an entirely different meaning.

As we became more sophisticated and familiar with the way of life in the U.S., we shared several laughs at the many different experiences we had since we first arrived as young, innocent girls from Ireland.

The Irish people brought with them the great gift of their Catholic faith as well as a litany of expressions regularly used to succinctly describe either a person or a situation back home. Indeed, the two enduring gifts my parents imparted to us children were a rock-solid religious faith and an enduring sense of humor. For example, when a mature person did something foolish you would hear, "There's no fool like an old fool." If someone was bemoaning not having a better life or missing out on something, the response to him would be "What you never had, you never missed" or "What never made you laugh will never make you cry." When food was in short supply, we often heard "A half a loaf is better than no bread." If you were not self-sufficient, you were told "It's a poor chicken that can't scratch for itself." Of course, you were judged by the company you kept. That was summed up with the saying "Birds of a feather flock together" or "Water reaches its own level." When a bachelor finally decided to marry, you would hear "Every old sock finds an old shoe" or "There's a lid for every pot." A cheapskate or penny pincher was described as someone who still "Had his or her First Communion money," or would "Mind mice at a crossroads." Maybe he would even "Live under a Hen" or "Skin a flea for the hide." A big shot was described as "A penny looking down on tuppence." When anyone was suspected of telling a tall tale, or acted as an authority on a certain issue, you heard "He's too sweet to be wholesome," or "He knows as much about the issue as a dog does about his father." Of course, there were many other expressions and adages that were equally appropriate and frequently used—bad cess to them all.

In addition to the many clichés, there was also a list of superstitions to prevent bad luck. Common among them were "Never open an umbrella indoors." "Don't put your shoes higher than your feet." "Never put your hat on the bed." "Always leave a house by the same door you entered it." "Don't break a mirror." That was the worst and most dreaded of all. If you had the misfortune to break a mirror, it meant seven years of bad luck were in store. If you spilled salt, you automatically picked up a pinch and threw it over your right shoulder with the danger that if you didn't, you would have a fight with someone. We were often warned not to be either too sure of ourselves or the outcome of a particular situation with the adage "Don't count your chickens 'til the eggs are hatched." Upon reading written material, we were well-advised to remember "Paper never refused ink," meaning you shouldn't believe everything you read. Those were among the most common expressions used that now come to mind.

As the years passed, I got on with my life in the U.S. I never forgot my home and family back in Ireland and longed for the day when I could afford to make a trip back again to see them all. That place I called home was truly just that—it was in my soul. I longed for letters from home with all the local news. When I had saved up enough money for airfare to make my first return trip three years after I came to the U.S., I was filled with excitement and joy at the thought of going home once again. It was an emotionally charged reunion, and it was wonderful to see my parents, brothers, and sisters once again. When I arrived at our house, my mother was crying, my father's eyes were teary, and my brothers and sisters were also filled with emotion. I was a little concerned as to why everyone was weepy at my arrival, but my mother put me at ease saying they were tears of joy.

When I immigrated to the U.S. in 1957 it was deemed a one-way trip. At that time, people rarely came back home once they left. It was very expensive and time-consuming to sail on the Cunard Line from New York to Queenstown, County Cork, and then travel by train to the closest hometown destination. This was often an additional overnight trek. Trans-Atlantic travel by air at that time was in its infancy and was an option reserved for the wealthy. The convenience of air travel did not become an affordable alternative until several years later when Aer Lingus, the airline of Ireland, opened up its trans-Atlantic route between Shannon and New York. This new service made trips to Ireland more attractive and introduced the traveler to experience Ireland the moment he boarded the plane to the lilt of Irish music and songs. Air travelers often reported they felt as though they were in Ireland as soon as they boarded the plane, before it ever left the runway in New York.

When someone returned home, it was a highly charged emotional occasion for both the immigrant and his family. The house was prepared and the favorite foods appeared. Indeed, the returnee was openly welcomed by family, friends, and neighbors. Vacationing or returning American family members and relatives were more the exception than the norm in those days and so no effort was spared to welcome them home. With the availability of air travel, Americans nowadays frequently include a trip to Ireland in their vacation or sightseeing plans. Conversely, in this 21st century, it is also not unusual for

Irish people to visit New York to trade stocks, conduct business, shop, play golf, and avail themselves of the current, favorable currency rate of exchange.

Unfortunately, much has been lost in the transition from those days when I looked forward to getting a letter in the familiar and handsome penmanship of my mother's hand. Today's e-mail messages and telephone calls will never replace the warmth and feeling she so well expressed in her own handwritten words. The art of letter writing has fallen by the wayside, replaced by electronic messaging and mass media.

I got married in 1961, in St. Augustine's Catholic Church, 6th Avenue, Brooklyn, to a first-generation, Irish-American man whose parents hailed from County Cork. Our wedding was very different from many of the weddings I had attended in New York. My parents had not yet met my new husband, my father did not give me away, and the band did not play "Daddy's Little Girl" at the reception. However, we were all united in love through telegrams from my family in Ireland filled with sentimental messages and emotional best wishes. My family would meet my husband through the medium of wedding photographs just as soon as they were developed and mailed.

Following our wedding, I moved from Brooklyn to the northwest Bronx, where my husband and I lived for a few years until we moved to our first home in Yonkers, New York. While this house was my permanent home, home for me was still that place back there in Leitrim where I had roots, where I could find refuge and comfort, where everything was familiar and a person could chat with friends and neighbors with ease. Going home was an occasion for me to return to myself and affirm who I was and what I believed, where conversation with the local farmers evolved around the weather, the land, and the price of cattle and livestock. The women were more interested in discussing the price of turkeys, eggs, clothing, and groceries, as well as the cost of living and raising a family. Home is that special place in the heart that is the center of who we are for it represents where our parents nourished us both spiritually and physically. It's difficult to know if the heart can be in more than one place.

> It's there we often grumble
> It's there we're glad to rest
> And when we've had trouble
> It's there we're treated best.
> —Anonymous

In 1965, a touch of home came to New York in the person of my father. He made his first trip to the U.S. to visit my two sisters and myself and to see his two surviving sisters who had emigrated more than forty years earlier. One sister had made a trip to Ireland in 1935; the other never went back since she left in the 1920s. That was the first time he had seen them since then. It was indeed an emotional and memorable reunion filled with tears, hugs, and reminiscences.

While my father was visiting me, a distant cousin of his died. He was interested in going to his wake and becoming re-acquainted with some of the distant relatives he had not seen since his boyhood. Wakes and weddings were occasions to renew acquaintance with relatives and friends. The deceased cousin was laid out in splendor in Walter B. Cooke's Funeral Home—a short distance from where I lived at that time. Together, my father and I walked to the wake and paid our respects.

When we returned home from the wake, he was filled with amazement and chit chat about how wakes are conducted in the U.S. He was indeed a very practical man gifted with a perceptive mind, an attentive ear, and a wonderful sense of humor.

Having seen how the deceased was dressed and prepared for burial, he considered it a total waste of the good suit, white shirt, and patterned tie his cousin was laid out in. He said, "There's many a man alive today who would be only too happy to wear those clothes to a happy event instead of to his grave." He asked, "What's the point in having someone all dressed up when he has no place to go?" In addition, he was shocked at how long dead people reposed, saying, "Are they turning them into bacon, or what?" And to his utter amazement, he was completely astonished to notice the deceased was wearing glasses, saying, "Do they think his vision is going to recover?" While musing to himself, he asked, "I wonder if they put the newspaper and a few dollars in his pocket as well." As he was going on and on, he half-audibly said, "Believe me, they're half mad in this country, or is this whole thing some kind racket? I can't wait to tell the neighbors back home about this so-called wake, or is it a debut? They won't believe me, I'm afraid, but I'll let you know their reaction and I guarantee it won't be much different from my own."

He was indeed mystified by American wakes, the velvet-lined casket and its matching pillow. When a person died back home, he or she was truly dead. They did not pass away. They were buried in a coffin in a graveyard; not placed in a casket and interred in a cemetery. The body, the corpse, not the remains, was dressed in a brown shroud and the wake was held in the house the first night. The afternoon following the death, the undertaker arrived at the house with the hearse and coffin. The body was taken to the parish church, where it remained overnight. Our local undertaker's horsedrawn hearse was a glass-paneled coach drawn by a team of horses. On the way to the house of the deceased, the driver wore regular street attire, but, on his way from the house to the church, he wore a white surplice over a long black cassock, a black sash draped over his shoulder, and a black top hat.

As the hearse passed people along the road on its way to church, they immediately knew by the way the driver was dressed that a removal was taking place and there was a body in the coffin inside the hearse. When they heard the clap of the horse's hooves approaching, they immediately came to a standstill, waited until the procession came into view, and stood with heads bowed until the funeral passed. It was customary in our part of Ireland in those days to let the funeral procession pass you—you never passed a funeral. Following the funeral Mass the day after the removal, burial took place in the nearby graveyard. In Ireland in those days embalming was unheard of, whereas in the U.S. it was necessary because it was not unusual to hold a two or three-day wake, sometimes longer, to accommodate out-of-town family members or relatives who needed the time to make appropriate travel arrangements.

While sitting on the couch in our living room, my father shared his firsthand experience of an American wake with my husband. He wondered at the words used to describe death. To him, a dead body was a corpse, a coffin was where the body was placed (casket was a new word to him), and people were buried in a graveyard. In desperation, he asked "Are they any less dead here than they are in Ireland?"

While we were gathered in our living room following the post-mortem on his cousin's wake, my father got up from the couch and moved to one of the armchairs. He sat there for a little while and then walked haltingly and contemplatively around the room as if he was distracted by something. He seemed to be pensive and preoccupied while trying to decide where he was most comfortable. Finally, after much moving around, he said "I just can't get comfortable in this room." I asked him, "Why was that?" I knew the couch and the armchairs were quite comfortable and I couldn't imagine why he was so restless. He turned to me and said, "There's nothing to face in this room." Not quite understanding what he meant, I asked him to explain. He said he was so accustomed to sitting facing the fireplace back home that he could not adapt to a room without a fireplace saying, "This room has no personality; I like to sit facing a fireplace." To him, a sitting room without a fireplace was not conducive to the kind of relaxation and comfortable conversation that were so much a part of his life. The fireplace in our large kitchen back home was the centerpiece of the room. It was the focal point where family, neighbors, and friends gathered and it always exuded an inviting as well as a comfortable, lived-in feeling. In front of the fireplace was where the topics of the day were discussed, family news and activities aired and shared, newspapers read, ghost stories told, and where sharing and remembering traditional ways were revisited and reflected upon.

In addition, it was around the fire that we children knelt down with our parents every evening to say the rosary while the glow from the embers kept our feet warm. It was truly the social center and heart of the home around which the entire household assembled in both joyful and sorrowful times. Oftentimes, it was not unusual for a member of the family to nod off to sleep half mesmerized by the crackling of the peat in front of the warm, cozy fire while it burned in the hearth.

One of my happiest memories is of my trip home accompanied by my husband and our four-year-old daughter—my parents' first grandchild. By now, I was married a little over six years, but this would be the first time my brothers and sisters met my husband and daughter. Together, we had a great time meeting relatives, friends, and neighbors, and renewing old acquaintances. My parents showered lots of attention on their first granddaughter and she enjoyed them very much. Both she and my husband were very happy to have an opportunity to spend time with grandparents, and the rest of my family, whom they had known through stories and photographs.

Five years after that happy occasion, I made another trip. This time it was the trip most people dread. The occasion was the sudden death of my father. When I arrived at Dublin Airport, following an overnight flight from New York, I was met upon arrival by one of my brothers. My mother, brothers, and sisters had assembled at my sister's house and together we went to view his body as he lay in repose at the foot of the altar in the small chapel of St. Vincent's Hospital. This was truly a moving hospital visit and experience. The hospital administrator, a nun, greeted us warmly and sympathetically and accompanied us to the small chapel where he was reposing:

> I saw him to the last, the grey
> Casting of the face,

157

The crabbed hands like this
Yielding to the cluster of the Rosary;
—Padraic Fallon

It was a sad trip, indeed, compounded by the fact that
he died in the cold month of December, shortly before
Christmas. To my dismay, my mother was a rock of
strength for all of us, even though she had not herself
fully recovered from the great shock of his sudden passing. She was a woman of such great faith, and she
accepted the will of God without question.

A few years after that trip, my family and I made
another trip. By this time my mother and siblings had
adjusted to my father's absence in and around the house,
but, since this was my first trip back since his death, I
deeply missed his presence and often found myself looking out the window thinking I would catch a glimpse of
him crossing through the fields or hear him coming
through the back door for his dinner. I felt the house was
terribly empty without him. My brother, who had inherited the farm, was doing a wonderful job of carrying on
his traditions as well as tending to the livestock and farm
just as he would have wanted.

Roughly ten years later, I went back to Ireland once
again. This was the saddest trip of all. It marked the very
sudden and untimely death of my sister, the one that had
pleurisy earlier in her life; the one who lived and worked
near me in Dublin; the one that went shopping with me;
the one whose picture was taken with me when we
walked across O'Connell Bridge wearing our new coats.
Thanks for all those wonderful memories, dearly
departed sister, beloved wife and gentle mother, named
Kathleen. She responded to God's command when He
sang that beautiful Irish melody "I'll Take You Home

Again, Kathleen" and made heaven her home.

Unfortunately, while she was coming out of the anesthesia following surgery she developed a cerebral hemorrhage and died. As is often said, "The operation was a success, but the patient died." At the time of her death, her children ranged in age from five to seventeen years. Three were under ten years of age and three teenagers. They were all at an age where they very much needed their mother; sadly that was not in the plan.

Her broken-hearted husband assumed total responsibility for their home and children. He did a yeoman's job of running the household and raising the children. Today, they are all responsible adults carrying on in the rich tradition imbued in them from birth by loving parents. Four of them are happily married and keeping busy raising their own young families. The remaining two are working in challenging positions in academia and business. They live in and around the city of Dublin where their father, now grandfather, enjoys their adult company and the gift of several grandchildren.

My sister's passing dealt a severe blow to her family and to my mother as well. I recall my mother saying she would have been delighted to trade places with Kathleen because she was the one with a young family and was needed most. Yet, in her unshakable faith, grief, and tears, she accepted the will of God graciously. Later on in her own life my mother suffered from a minor form of diabetes. She never liked going to the doctor. As a matter of fact, when she entered his office, her heart would race and her blood pressure would skyrocket. While she feared what the doctor might tell her, she had an even greater fear of ever having to be admitted to a hospital. She suffered from a severe dread of white-itis and a very real fear of hospitals.

Following my father's death, my mother continued to live at home with my youngest brother, taking care of the household duties as well as his needs. She loved flowers and gardening and was blessed with a very successful and productive green thumb. One day, in late fall, she did not feel her usual self. My brother called for the doctor to come to the house and check on her condition. Fearing she needed more medical assistance than he could provide, he arranged for an ambulance to take her to the hospital. On her way to the hospital, she died peacefully in that ambulance. She had been granted her wish and saved from her fear of ever having to be admitted to a hospital. Regrettably, I was unable to go to her funeral because the airports in the northeastern part of the U.S. were closed due to Gloria, a violent hurricane that made landfall at that time. I remember my beloved mother fondly and dearly and with deep regret that I was not able to attend her funeral due to circumstances beyond my control.

My trips to Ireland nowadays are much more pleasant. I go there to attend weddings of either nieces or nephews, to relax and enjoy the scenic, Irish countryside, to keep in touch with my roots, and to share in the positive frame of mind and better living conditions enjoyed by all as a result of the recent dramatic progress in the currently fast-growing Irish economy—The Celtic Tiger.

Having been blessed with two talented and loving daughters myself, I was a full-time, stay-at-home mother. That was the accepted way of life at that time. As a rule, the mother stayed home and raised the children while the father worked to provide for the family. Daycare and full-time child care were not options then. When our daughters were in school, I became involved in church events, their school and education, local and civic activities, and always maintained a love of learning.

When my older daughter was in her senior year of high school, I went to work at Fordham University and pursued my college education in the evenings. It was a daunting challenge taking the subway from mid-Manhattan to the Bronx following a day's work to attend three-hour classes three, and sometimes four nights a week. Nevertheless, I struggled onward and graduated with a B.A. degree, majoring in both philosophy and business. I had finally accomplished the goal that I had set for myself and was delighted that I had pursued my dream.

My older daughter and I graduated from Fordham University on the same day. It was with a sense of pride, accomplishment, and sentimentality that we presented each other with our degrees. She was a full-time day student, and I was a full-time evening student. In the history of the university, founded in 1841, it was one of the few occasions, if not the only one, when a mother and daughter graduated on the same day. She met her future husband during their college days at Fordham. A year after her graduation they got married. Following his graduation from Fordham Preparatory School and Fordham University, he completed a J.D. at Pace University School of Law. They currently live in southern Dutchess County, a little over sixty miles north of Yonkers. They are the parents of three children: one boy, a freshman in Seton Hall University; and two girls, a high school junior and an elementary school student. While her children were in school during the day, my daughter returned to college, on a full-time basis, to pursue a degree in nursing. Against odds and obstacles, as well as the demands of running a home, attending to homework, PTA meetings, teaching religious education, volunteering on parish council committees as well as local and civic organizations, she recently fulfilled the program's requirements and graduated as a Professional Registered Nurse. Hooray! Well done indeed! Warmest congratulations.

My younger daughter got married following her graduation from Fordham University in 1990. She and her husband, a graduate of the United States Military Academy at West Point, lived in Germany for a few years. Following that military assignment, they returned to the U.S. where he served as a captain in the U.S. Army at Fort Sill, Oklahoma. At the present time they live in Illinois, a short distance from Chicago. They are the parents of three children, one girl and two boys—two in elementary school and one in junior high school.

I recently retired following more than twenty years' employment at Fordham University. As I write this memoir, my husband and I are very much enjoying our extended family and our six grandchildren. We both look forward to our next trip to Ireland. As we plan our future, we dream of treating ourselves to a retirement escape, living out our remaining years, *Deo Volente,* in a warmer clime away from the harsh, cold winters of the northeast.

We are grateful to God for the gift of good health, a warm loving family, loyal and trusted friends, and the many blessings bestowed upon us across the years. As I look back on my early childhood in Leitrim, my teenage years in Dublin, and both my young adult and adult years in the United States, I am happy to say it's been a great trip, a happy, simple life filled with love, faith, sacrifice, humor, laughter, and an occasional tear shed along the way, which we were prepared for since that day in 1961 when we were forewarned in our marriage ceremony that we took each other for better or for worse, confident that God would not serve us more than we could handle. Memories linger and are rekindled when I hear Larry Cunningham's poignant rendition of "Lovely Leitrim":

Last night I had a pleasant dream
I woke up with a smile
I dreamt that I was back again
In dear old Erin's isle
I thought I saw Lough Allen's banks
In the valleys down below
Sure, t'was My Lovely Leitrim
Where the Shannon waters flow
—P. Fitzpatrick